Thre
of
Destiny

Embracing Responsibility with Compassion

By
Gerard Conway

MAPLE
PUBLISHERS

Threads of Destiny (Embracing Responsibility with Compassion)

Author: Gerard Conway

Copyright © Gerard Conway (2024)

The right of Gerard Conway to be identified as author of this work has been asserted by the author in accordance with section 77 and 78 of the Copyright, Designs and Patents Act 1988.

First Published in 2024

ISBN 978-1-83538-182-3 (Paperback)
    978-1-83538-183-0 (E-Book)

Cover Design and Book Layout by:
    White Magic Studios
    www.whitemagicstudios.co.uk

Published by:
    Maple Publishers
    Fairbourne Drive, Atterbury,
    Milton Keynes,
    MK10 9RG, UK
    www.maplepublishers.com

CONTENTS

Preface

"I invite readers to reflect on their own journeys and embrace the interconnectedness of our lives. 'Threads of Destiny: Embracing Responsibility with Compassion' serves as a testament to the power of empathy, offering a guiding light for those facing their own trials and tribulations, and a never give up attitude."

Gerard Conway

Autobiography

Introduction

"Threads of Destiny: Embracing Responsibility with Compassion" takes readers on a heartfelt journey through the life of Gerard Conway, a man shaped by his life's experiences.

What unfolds is a compelling story that extends beyond the individual journey to touch the universal aspects of the human experience. Gerard, with a profound understanding of the intricacies of life, invites readers to embark on a reflective journey through his own life story, which illustrates the interconnectedness of our shared existence.

In the pages of "Threads of Destiny, I share my personal triumphs and tribulations, offering a window into the complexities of my experiences.

My story is not just a chronicle of events but a demonstration of the power of empathy and compassion.

As readers navigate through the chapters, they find themselves drawn into the emotional landscape of my life, discovering the threads that connect us all.

The title, "Threads of Destiny", suggests a deeper exploration of the closely connected nature of our lives, highlighting the invisible ties that bind us together. My story becomes a metaphorical loom, weaving together the fabric of my life.

Through my words, I implore readers to recognise the impact of their own actions on the greater tapestry of humanity.

"Embracing Responsibility with Compassion" emerges as a central theme, guiding readers to contemplate the significance of shouldering responsibilities with a compassionate heart.

My journey becomes a beacon of inspiration for those facing their own trials and tribulations. The story does not shy away from the challenges I encountered but instead emphasises a resilient spirit—a "never give up" attitude that becomes a rallying cry for those navigating their own paths.

As readers delve into "Threads of Destiny," they are not merely observers but active participants in the shared human experience. My story becomes a source of guidance and encouragement, to embolden individuals to approach life's challenges with empathy, responsibility, and a commitment to persevere. In the end, my autobiography serves as a reminder that our individual stories are creating a richer, more vibrant tapestry of shared destiny.

Born on April 14th 1956, Gerard reflects on the intricate tapestry of his existence. Exploring how the events and responsibilities he encountered moulded his character.

"I never could have imagined that my life's journey would take me through such incredible highs and devastating lows. As I sit here reflecting, I look back on the events that have shaped me into the person I am today. I feel that I am compelled to share my story."

Born into a world of uncertainty, my early years were marked by constant change.

Growing up in poverty, in England, and orphaned at the age of 11, I was struck down with a life-threatening illness, which took my Dad away from us, and surviving a near fatal car accident, I have learned to adapt and find solace in the fleeting moments of stability.

From an incredibly early age, I yearned for security, and a sense of belonging that seemed perpetually out of reach. It was this longing that drove me forward, pushing me to work tirelessly and strive for a life beyond the confines of my circumstances.

With determination as my driver, I embarked on a path filled with both triumphs and tribulations. Fifty years of hard work defined my existence as I carved out a place in the world.

I discovered hidden wellsprings of strength within myself, navigating homelessness, and the unforgiving streets and seeking refuge in the most unlikely places.

In the chapters that follow, I recount the captivating and harrowing events that unfolded during that time. From the casinos of the high seas to the deceitful promises that lured me into ill-fated investments, my journey took an unexpected detour into a world of betrayal, financial ruin, and heartache, which cost me and my family everything we owned. While it is challenging to compare these different experiences, it is crucial to acknowledge that each one represented a significant hardship and trauma.

As I recount these pivotal moments and the lessons they imparted, I invite you, dear reader, to join me on this voyage of self-discovery. Together, we will navigate the turbulent waters that threatened to engulf me and emerge on the shores of hope and redemption.

This is not just the story of my life; it is a testament to the indomitable human spirit—a demonstration that even in the face of adversity, we can find the strength to rise, rebuild, and embrace life's unexpected twists and turns.

The belief I hold is that every person possesses the potential to achieve success in life, regardless of the challenges they might face. It is my conviction that no matter your background, upbringing, or current situation, there is an inherent capacity within us all to overcome obstacles and achieve goals.

This belief encourages a positive outlook on life, for people's potential, emphasising that everyone has the capacity to create a better future for themselves. It promotes the idea that circumstances do not define a person's destiny; rather, it is their determination, efforts, and belief in their own abilities that pave the way for success.

"In the chapters that follow, I will peel back the layers of my existence, baring my soul and sharing the triumphs and heartaches that have shaped me. I hope that my journey will inspire you, challenge you, and remind you that within each of us lies the power to overcome even the darkest of days."

⊷⊶⟨⟩⊷⊶

Chapter 1

The Burden of Duty

As I explore the concept of responsibility and its weight on my shoulders, I candidly share the triumphs and struggles I faced as I navigated the unpredictable twists of life. I learned that circumstances could dictate our choices. The sacrifices made and the decisions taken were not always easy, but my unwavering commitment to empathy drove me forward.

Step into my world, where the concept of responsibility was not just a word – it was a heavyweight contender in the ring of life. Pull up a seat, because I am about to draw back the curtain on the trials, tribulations, and, yes, the occasional triumphs of carrying the weight of duty on my shoulders.

So, picture this: life is like a roller coaster with more loops and turns than a maze. And right in the front seat, I am gripping the handles, ready for whatever fate decides to throw at me.

Responsibilities? Oh God, they were like the extra baggage I never asked for but ended up carrying anyway.

The journey was a mix of victories and so many challenges. It is like fate decided to play a game with me, and I found myself holding the bag of responsibilities with no lifeline to call. But hey, life is not a bed of roses; it is more like a series of "you-didn't-see-that-coming" plot twists.

Circumstances? Yes, they can be real pain in the arse sometimes. They barged in like uninvited guests at a party and forced me to make choices I never thought I would face. It was like playing chess with life, and just when I thought I had it all figured out, the rules changed.

Sacrifices? Oh, I made them, like an expert juggler trying to keep all the balls in the air.

Decisions? They were like darts thrown blindfolded, hoping they had hit the target and not some innocent bystander.

But here is the real master– empathy.

It became my secret weapon, my guiding star through the chaos. It was like I had a superpower that urged me to keep moving forward, even when the path was murky, and the decisions weighed a ton. Empathy became my compass, reminding me that every choice I made had consequences, not just for me but for the world around me.

So, there you have it – my tale of wrestling with responsibility, a heavyweight opponent that can knock you down as easily as it can lift you up. Triumphs were sweeter, struggles were tougher, and through it all, I kept moving forward, driven by the unwavering commitment to understanding, compassion, and a stubborn refusal to be defeated by life's unexpected turns.

Chapter 2

The Price of Sacrifice

At times, the path forward seemed clear, the choices easily made. But often, the lines blurred, and I found myself grappling with the weight of responsibility, torn between personal fulfilment and the obligations I felt towards my family. Not forgetting the promise, I made to my Mom as she lay dying beside me.

The toll of these choices was not lost on me. There were moments of weariness when the weight that I was about to carry threatened to buckle my resolve. In those moments,

I discovered a wellspring of resilience within, a deep-rooted strength that propelled me forward.

Navigating Life's Tightrope

Life, the ultimate expert in throwing curveballs when you least expect them. Welcome to my world, where balancing personal desires and the needs of others became a high-stake tightrope act that even the most fearless circus performer would envy.

Imagine this: there I was, on that precarious tightrope, every step filled with the possibility of triumph or sacrifice. Think of it like walking a tightrope over a pit of lions, except the lions are life choices and they are not all that cuddly.

However, Wait! There is a twist! My personal aspirations had a built-in crew – my brothers and sister. Yes, they were like my very own entourage, demanding attention, compassion, and a generous helping of selflessness. It was like they saw me as the all-knowing, all-fixing magician, and that was a heavy burden to take on.

Sometimes, the path ahead was as clear as day, the choices straightforward like a paved road. More often than not, it was like trying to read a map without glasses – everything blurred into a confusing mess. I was stuck in a tug-of-war between personal happiness and the gravitational pull of responsibilities to my loved ones.

Here is the real catch – the toll of those choices. There were days when exhaustion threatened to turn my determination into a river of doubt. Yet, in those moments of vulnerability, I discovered a resilience within me. It was like I had a secret superhero power, a tenacity that could rival even the most unyielding forces of nature.

My journey was a tightrope walk between personal dreams and family obligations, a balancing act. Triumphs felt sweeter, sacrifices felt heavier, and through it all, that deep-rooted strength propelled me onward. It is like life handed me a tightrope, and I decided to dance on it, even when the wind threatened to knock me off balance.

Chapter 3

Embracing Loss and Empathy

The inevitability — an understanding that someone had to step forward and fill the void left behind. This pivotal Moment etched a sense of duty on my soul, shaping the course of my life for over five decades. It was through empathy for others' experiences that I discovered the true meaning of responsibility, in providing support and guidance.

Let us rewind to those days leading up to the farewell to the one who meant the world to me – my much-loved Mom. It was like the universe whispered a sombre truth in my ear: someone had to step forward and fill the echoing void left behind. Inevitability was a heavy cloak, and I donned it, ready to face what lay ahead.

Then, like a thunderclap in the night, came that pivotal Moment. The Moment that etched a sense of duty onto my soul, a commitment that would mould my life's journey. It was as if the stars had aligned, and the universe decided it was my turn to carry the torch of responsibility.

Empathy was my secret weapon, my guiding light through the fog of loss. It was like I stumbled upon a treasure chest of understanding, and I could not help but share its riches. Empathy became the lens through which I viewed the world, transforming my sense of duty into a heartfelt mission to support and guide others.

You see, this is not just a story – it is an exploration of the human condition, a journey through the difficulties of emotion that make us who we are. It is like I am inviting you to take a front-row seat to my life's roller coaster, with empathy as the safety net that keeps us grounded amidst the loops and drops.

As you read the pages, you will find firsthand experiences woven with threads of understanding, a deep dive into the ocean of human emotions. It is like I have handed you a compass to navigate the complexities of life, using empathy as the North Star that guides us through uncharted waters.

So, fasten your seatbelt and prepare to embark on a journey within, loss, and the unwavering quest for understanding – they are all here, waiting to be discovered, page by page, in the intricate story of my life.

Chapter 4

Discovering that I had a Twin

The life-altering experience of discovering my twin brother, at the age of 18 months old, had a profound and lasting impact on me from the beginning.

The entrance of my identical twin brother into the world was like a cosmic revelation that there was, indeed, someone else out there who looked exactly like me. It was like stumbling upon a real-life mirror image of myself in a parallel universe, a doppelgänger who happened to be walking around in a different body. Not only did he replicate my physical appearance, but there was also the tantalising possibility that he shared some of my quirks and idiosyncrasies.

Fast-forward through toddlerhood, and there we were, two peas in a pod, tackling the world together like a dynamic duo. It was like having a lifelong teammate, except instead of fighting villains, we were taking on life's challenges. Our shared experiences became the bricks that built the foundation of a unique sibling bond.

Growing up, we were more than just brothers – we were confidants with secret handshakes and inside jokes that could rival any stand-up comedian's routine. Our shared history turned into a treasure trove of stories, a collection of adventures that made us comrades-in-arms in the battle of self-discovery.

Our twinship became a safety net, a source of belonging and comfort amid the uncertainties of life. Through thick and thin, we leaned on each other, a bond that held steady even in the face of our parents' absence.

This connection is like an unbreakable silk thread, woven through the tapestry of our lives. We weathered storms together, celebrated victories, and tackled growing pains side by side. It was like having an in-built companion, a partner who shared my past and understood the depths of my journey.

Our journey, oh what a ride it has been! Moments of synchrony mixed with individual growth, shaping our identities like clay in the hands of destiny. That twin bond acted as a rudder, guiding us through the choppy waters of adolescence and the perplexing maze of adulthood.

As the pages of my life continue to turn, my twin's presence remains a constant, a light guiding me through the uncharted territory of existence. Our journey is a reminder that sometimes, the most extraordinary connections are right under our noses – or, in this case, right in the cot next to us.

⸺⸻◇⸻⸺

Chapter 5

A Journey through Dark and Light

Desperation to Resilience

Picture a young soul grappling with the weight of the world on fragile shoulders that was me, standing on the edge of an abyss of desperation, where the ground seemed to crumble beneath me. Life's challenges had mounted like an insurmountable tower, and I found myself at a crossroads – succumbing to the darkness.

The journey from desperation to resilience was not linear. It was a dance between setbacks and progress, tears and triumphs. There were moments when I stumbled and moments when I soared. And through it all, I discovered the strength within me that I never knew existed.

Growing up in the Birmingham area of England, where I was raised in a working-class family.

Shaped by the struggles and strength of my parents, (Thomas and Agnes). I vividly recount the challenging circumstances they faced after arriving in Birmingham, England, as penniless immigrants from Ireland in the 1950s.

Irish immigrants have a long history in England, dating back centuries.

My Mom and Dad experienced racial prejudice when they first arrived in England, they were turned away by landlords who displayed visual signs on their doors saying no Irish or blacks.

They formed tight-knit communities in cities like Liverpool, Manchester, Birmingham and London. They often faced overcrowded and squalid living conditions in areas known as "Irish slums". They also encountered prejudice and discrimination. They were sometimes blamed for various social problems, including crime and disease.

Anti-Irish sentiment was fuelled by stereotypes and political tensions, particularly in relation to Irish nationalism.

Despite discrimination, many Irish immigrants found work in the growing industrial and construction sectors of England. They played a significant role in building the infrastructure of England's cities. My Dad was one of those.

It is important to recognise that the experiences of Irish immigrants in England have been diverse. While many faced adversity and discrimination, others successfully integrated into British society and contributed to the country's culture and economy. Over time, the Irish community has become an integral part of the multicultural fabric of England.

Mom and Dad's desire to integrate into England's culture with their Irish background reflected their determination to adapt to their new environment and provide a better life for us all as a family.

Like many immigrants, my Mom and Dad left Ireland in search of better economic prospects. They understood that England offered more job opportunities and a chance to escape the economic hardships of rural Ireland. By seeking employment and financial stability in England, my Dad aimed to provide a comfortable life for his growing family.

To integrate into English society, my parents would have respected and adhered to local customs.

Active participation in local religious and social activities fostered a sense of belonging. My Mom and Dad attended the local catholic church to help them build relationships and become part of the social fabric of their new home.

Embracing Multiculturalism: While striving to integrate into English culture, Mom and Dad maintained a connection to their Irish roots. This balance between embracing their Irish heritage and integrating into English society showcased their ability to navigate multiculturalism and celebrate both aspects of their identity.

Despite the limited financial means, our parents instilled in all of us an intense sense of discipline and values rooted in "Victorian Principles". While the household was strict, there was an undeniable undercurrent of love that permeated our family.

As a child, I was one of eight, I witnessed my Mom and Dad's unwavering dedication to us as children, and our well-being. Dad worked tirelessly to provide for us all, trying to ensure that basic needs were met despite the challenges he faced. Mom kept a good, clean, and loving home for us all.

My experience of living in poverty paints a vivid picture of the challenging conditions we had to endure. The overcrowded living situation, where four of us shared a bed and relied on old overcoats for warmth, highlighted the lack of necessities and the limited resources available to us.

Where we lived was no ordinary dwelling. It bore the echoes of merry nights, hearty laughter, and the clinking of glasses and the stale stench of alcohol that lingered in the carpeting and furnishings from its past as a public house. Stepping into this space felt like stepping into a time capsule, where history breathed life into our everyday existence.

The heart of the old public house – its former pub area – was now our living room. The long bar had transformed into a sturdy wooden table around which we gathered for meals. The original mirrors behind the bar, still adorned with a touch of vintage elegance, reflected not just our images, but also the stories of patrons long gone.

The fusion of past and present was evident in every "nook and cranny". The fireplace, once a gathering spot for locals seeking warmth and friendship, now provided comfort for our family on chilly evenings. The original wooden beams overhead embraced the stories of generations. Our furniture was made up of a few chairs and a sideboard.

Each bedroom felt like a sanctuary. The walls whispered tales of the pub's guests as we lay down to sleep, the floorboards creaking underfoot as if sharing secrets. The windows, framing views of the ever-changing English skies, connected us to the world outside as they once connected patrons to the streets.

The rough cold winters we experienced as children, further emphasised the harshness of our daily living conditions. As the temperatures dropped outside, the bitter cold crept its way into every corner of the house, making it feel like there was no escape from its grasp.

That thick frost on the inside of the windows was a stark visual reminder of the severe conditions endured during those winter months. It served as a barrier between the interior of the house, and the outside world, insolating us inside from the freezing winds and snow-covered back streets beyond. The frosty patterns on the glass obscured any view of the outside, creating an almost claustrophobic feeling as the days grew shorter and darker.

In an attempt to stay warm, makeshift insulation was often employed, with blankets and layers of clothing placed around doors and windows to prevent the cold air from seeping in. But despite these efforts, the icy chill still managed to find its way inside, chilling our very bones. Those freezing temperatures made even the simplest tasks, like getting out of bed in the morning, and washing ourselves feel like daunting challenges. It was difficult to muster the energy to face the day, and the desire to stay wrapped in warm covers was a constant battle against the necessity to deal with daily responsibilities.

I remember during those hard frosty winter mornings, finding ways to keep warm had become a priority. Heating sources, often limited or inadequate, were cherished commodities. Gathering around a crackling fire, a couple of days a week, provided a brief respite from the biting cold, but it was a luxury that could not be sustained for long periods.

Despite the hardship, the winters also brought a sense of camaraderie and togetherness as we huddled close for warmth, sharing stories and laughter to distract from the harsh reality outside. Surviving those winters required strength, resilience, and a collective effort to make it through, fostering bonds that would withstand the challenges of the seasons. They left an indelible mark on the memories of all of us who endured them.

The scarcity of heating, with coal being a luxury, reveals the struggles we faced to maintain warmth and comfort in the house. We had no money to buy coal, so my brothers and I would chase after the "Coal Lorry" as it went down the lane. We would collect the bits of coal and slack off the ground as it fell off. Often, even with the threat of the driver giving me a good hiding, I would jump up on the back of the lorry and raid the bags. Sometimes if we were lucky there would be enough to light a whole fire for an evening. We had to prioritise our limited resources for essential needs such as food and other basic expenses, leaving little room for heating the house adequately.

Enduring such cold and uncomfortable conditions posed significant physical health and emotional challenges, especially during the winter months, which would eventually take its toll on the whole family.

Poverty shaped my perspective on life, from an early age, and instilled in me a strong drive to overcome adversity and improve my circumstances.

Although we lacked material wealth, my Mom and Dad's love for us was palpable, creating a nurturing environment amidst the modest circumstances. They taught me the value of resilience and determination, planting the seeds that would later drive me to overcome the obstacles I was to encounter in the future. They also instilled in me the belief that with dedication and a strong work ethic, one could achieve remarkable things regardless of their starting point.

While my time together with Mom and Dad was tragically cut short, I carried with me the memories of their love and the lessons they imparted throughout my journey. Their influence provided me with a moral compass and a sense of family bond that guided me.

The working-class background in which I was raised served as a foundation for my character. It instilled in me a deep appreciation for the value of hard-earned success and a determination to rise above all circumstances. The lessons learned were instrumental in my journey towards self-made success, as well as in my ability to weather the future storms that lay ahead.

Like lots of things in life, I did not know the full background of both Mom and Dad, and only learned after they passed away that my Dad's education and his career as a nurse in Ireland never contributed to the financial stability of our family. As he never got to practise in England. My Dad's decision to train as a male nurse was significant. In the mid-20th century, nursing was a profession that typically attracted more women than men. His choice to pursue nursing as a career was influenced by factors such as the demand for healthcare professionals in Ireland at the time.

Also, my Dad's ability to speak Gaelic fluently was a testament to his cultural heritage and linguistic skills. Gaelic, also known as Irish, is one of the official languages of Ireland and holds deep cultural significance.

His fluency in Gaelic was a connection to the rich cultural heritage of Ireland. Gaelic is not only a language but also a carrier of history, literature, and tradition. His ability to speak Gaelic should have allowed our family to maintain ties to Irish culture even while living in England. However, this was curtailed with the lack of Irish immigrants in their social circle.

His journey from Ireland to England, his education, and his choice of profession highlight the resilience and adaptability of immigrants. Moving to a new country, learning a new language, and pursuing a career in a foreign land are significant challenges. His ability to overcome these challenges is a testament to his determination and strength.

His commitment to education, as well as his connection to Irish culture, may have shaped our family's identity and priorities.

I wanted to incorporate these details into my autobiography to provide a richer understanding of my family's history and the diverse influences that shaped my upbringing. It also highlights the unique experiences and contributions of my Mom and Dad within the context of immigration and cultural adaptation.

Dad's decision to work in cable laying reflects his adaptability and determination to support the family in a new country. Like many immigrants, he had to make pragmatic choices to secure employment that was available to enable him to provide for our family's needs.

It is important to know the economic circumstances at the time.

Retraining in a different country can be costly and time-consuming. His choice to work in road construction as a cable layer may have been influenced by the need to provide a steady income without the financial burden of additional education.

My early memories are tinged with scarcity, as my Dad, Thomas, worked tirelessly on the roads, laying cables, often away from home for most of the week. It was during this time that a significant event etched itself into my memory—a trench collapsing on top of him. In a Moment that showcased both his resilience and dry sense of humour, Dad who was lying at the bottom of the collapsed trench, clearly badly hurt from the weight of clay and rubble covering him, responded defiantly to the ganger man's inquiry about the frame that was securing the trench. Dad's response was, "What about this fucking frame?"

The incident resulted in my Dad breaking both of his legs, which led to months of unemployment and severe financial hardship.

During those difficult months that followed, food became scarce, and I recall the distress and desperation that Mom endured. I often found her alone, crying. I would ask her if she was alright. She would put her hands on my face and tell me that she was fine and that things would get better soon. The memory of her anguish remains imprinted on my heart.

With my Dad convalescing at home, the wounds from his workplace accident went beyond the physical. He grappled with anger, frustration, and the changes in his life. The Dad we had known was turning before our eyes, and it was a transformation that shook the very foundation of our family.

Amidst this turmoil, a new demon emerged – addiction. The allure of the pub became a siren's call, an escape from the anguish and uncertainty that plagued him. The family allowance, meant to support our basic needs, often found its way into the till of the local pub.

The tensions in our home reached a fever pitch during these moments of desperation. Dad's anger would surge, and he would confront Mom in a violent, desperate manner. The shouts, the grabbing, and the demands for money became a harrowing pattern, leaving our family torn apart.

As a child, I found myself thrust into the eye of this storm. I could not bear to see my parents in such turmoil. I would step between them, my small body serving as a fragile shield against the tempest that raged. With tears in my eyes, I would beg them to stop, to find a way out of this cycle of despair.

As time passed and Dad's health improved, the violence started to subside. The scars of those turbulent times remained, etched into my memory. The family emerged from those difficult days with a deeper appreciation for the fragility of life and the strength of our connections.

The days leading on were not helped by the lack of resources and in particular the shortage of money to buy food to feed us. Mentally and emotionally, hunger became an all-consuming preoccupation. It was difficult to focus on anything else. My mind was fixed on finding a solution to this problem. The longing for food became overwhelming, it impacted all our moods and emotions.

I can recall the physical ache, and a deep sense of emptiness that was hard to ignore. That also brought on emotional pain, as the inability to satisfy this basic need led to feelings of helplessness, frustration and despair. Experiencing this chronic hunger, and the pain, made me think about where the next meal was coming from and how I could try and stop it for all of us. I was in a constant state of stress, but I was determined to do something about it.

Witnessing the struggles faced by Mom, brothers, and my sister, I felt an unexplained need to alleviate their hunger and hardship. Often seeing days when food was that scarce, my siblings would be rolling on the floor holding their stomachs in pain.

I decided, one morning, that I would go out and take milk and bread from doorsteps of other people's houses. I did it to take the hunger away for a day or two. This is something that I am not proud of, but needs must at that time!

As the early morning light cast long shadows across the dimly lit hallway of the towering high-rise, I found myself perched precariously on the eleventh floor, my heart pounding with desperation. With trembling hands, I reached out for the meagre sustenance of bread and milk, my only solace amidst the relentless hunger gnawing at my stomach.

But just as I dared to hope for a fleeting Moment of respite, the metallic click of a key turning in the latch shattered the silence like a thunderclap, sending a jolt of fear coursing through my veins. Frozen in place, I watched in horror as the door swung open, revealing a figure silhouetted against the harsh glare of the morning light.

Before I could react, a voice laced with venom sliced through the air like a dagger, piercing through the stillness with its ferocity. "Come here, you little bastard!" the man spat, his words dripping with contempt and rage. Every fibre of my being screamed at me to flee, to escape the wrath of this stranger whose fury threatened to consume me whole.

But there was nowhere to run, nowhere to hide from the accusatory glare burning into my soul. As I stood there, trembling and defenceless, I knew in that Moment that I was trapped, ensnared in a web of desperation and despair with no way out.

In the blink of an eye, the world around me blurred into a whirlwind of chaos and confusion, the cacophony of my racing heartbeat drowning out all other sound. With a sinking feeling in the pit of my stomach, I braced myself for whatever punishment awaited me, knowing deep down that I would not escape unscathed from this harrowing encounter.

As I stood frozen in terror, the man's eyes bore into mine with a searing intensity that seemed to strip away all pretence of innocence. With a sudden, savage motion, he raised his foot and delivered a forceful kick to my backside, sending me sprawling forward in a whirlwind of pain and disorientation.

The impact knocked the breath from my lungs and sent me careering towards the ground, the contents of my makeshift bag scattering across the unforgiving floor in a chaotic symphony of destruction. I watched in horror as the bottle of milk shattered upon impact, its white contents spilling out like a river of lost hope, staining the cold concrete with its silent lament.

For a Moment, time seemed to stand still as I lay there, dazed, and battered, with the echoes of the man's cruel laughter ringing in my ears like a relentless drumbeat of humiliation. But even as my body screamed in protest, a primal instinct kicked in, propelling me forward with a surge of adrenaline-fuelled determination.

With trembling limbs and a heart pounding like a drum in my chest, I scrambled to my feet and fled, each step a painful reminder of the brutality I had endured. Down eleven flights of stairs I raced, each descent a harrowing dive into the depths of despair, my breath coming in ragged gasps as I fought to outrun the spectre of my assailant's wrath.

But as I burst through the safety of the ground floor and into the cool embrace of the morning air, I felt a surge of triumph course through my veins, mingled with the bitter taste of fear and defeat. Though battered and bruised, I had escaped the clutches of my tormentor, my spirit unbroken and my resolve unwavering. I disappeared into the anonymity of the bustling city streets. I knew that though the scars of that fateful encounter may linger.

My mind turned to home and going back without the spoils. As luck would have it, I found another house that was able to provide us food for that day. I was more worried about the wrath I would encounter, from my brothers, if I was unable to deliver.

I wasn't aware that my Mom's sadness and helplessness were intertwined with the early stages of disease that would eventually claim her life so young. In the gallery of my memories, one portrait stands out with a brilliance that time cannot dim. Mom was a woman whose beauty extended far beyond her appearance, illuminating even the darkest corners of her journey.

She was a woman of striking grace, had a beauty that transcended the realm of physicality. Her raven-black hair framed a face that held the secrets of the universe. Her eyes, like deep pools of kindness, radiated a warmth that could envelop even the coldest hearts. Her smile, a beacon of hope, spoke volumes about the strength within her.

What truly set my Mom apart was her outlook on life. She possessed a happiness that wasn't fleeting or superficial; it was a deep-seated contentment that seemed to emanate from her very being. Even when faced with the gravity of a terminal illness, she embraced life with a spirit that refused to be dimmed. Her smile remained unwavering. It was a light that shone even in the darkest of times, it carried the weight of her battles, the sorrows she bore, and yet, it was an inspiration to all who knew her.

Her battle with the terminal illness showed her inner strength. She faced her journey with a courage that defied words, never allowing the gravity of her condition to diminish her zest for life. Her unwavering determination to live each day determined to take on the demon illness inside her was a lesson in embracing the present, regardless of the uncertainties of the future.

As time goes on, the memory of my Mom's radiance remains etched in my heart. Her beauty was not only in her physical form but in the grace with which she lived her life. Her outlook, her smile, her courage – they are the legacy she left behind.

And in the tapestry of my life, her spirit continues to weave a thread of inspiration, reminding me to find strength even in the midst of life's storms.

Every day of my early childhood was a challenge. During that period, we had to rely on a meagre family allowance as at times it was the sole source of income.

Another memory etched in my mind was the weekly ritual of Mom walking a considerable distance to the "Pawn Shop" on Mondays. She would pawn Dad's best suit and shoes to obtain half a crown, (12p today) just enough to buy bread to sustain us for a couple of days.

Eventually, my Dad was able to return to work, but his excessive drinking persisted. Each Thursday, after receiving his pay packet, Dad would head straight to the pub, (Often, we would not have had anything to eat on that day). It was then that I was driven by determination, and I would approach my intoxicated Dad, braving his anger and disappointment. Clinging to his trouser leg, shouting that Mom has sent me. I would implore him for money to buy essentials like bread, milk, and a few portions of chips and scratchings. The reluctant handover of money became a regular occurrence, as I sprinted back to my desperate Mom, racing against time to retrieve my Dad's suit and shoes from the pawn shop before he returned home.

Even at such an early age I had realised that this could not go on. There had to be a way of my brothers and me doing something to bring in money to the house.

Just up the road from our house was a wholesaler's business that shop keepers would get their groceries from. I had an idea that I might be able to earn some money by helping in some way. I decided that I had nothing to lose, so I sought casual work. I was aged 7 at the time. The name of the business was J & F's wholesalers. It was situated at the top of Queens Road, Aston, Birmingham.

I assisted shopkeepers in loading goods into their cars before school, earning a few pennies each time. It wasn't a lot of money, but it was something. (Most of the kind shopkeepers new that I could not really carry the heavy boxes, but they still allowed me to help. They saw a dishevelled figure, I was painfully thin and had very little strength.) Physically, my clothes were ill-fitting, suggesting a lack of attention to personal grooming and clothing maintenance.

We had no choice but to wear mismatched hand me downs.

One thing that my Mom was a stickler about was us washing ourselves every day from head to toe.

My posture and movements might have appeared to be sluggish or lethargic, conveying a sense of exhaustion and weariness. I had not eaten the day before. My face may have shown signs of fatigue, with dark circles under my eyes, and a hint of sadness or resignation in my eyes. I did not care about what people thought. These were desperate times, and my Mom was dying, and the future for us as a family was bleak.

As time went on and we were a little older, there were other things that all the older boys did to try and earn money. One of those things was minding cars, for supporters who went to football matches. We lived close to the football ground, and John my eldest brother allocated different streets that were geographically located between our house and Villa Park. I was given Electric Avenue in Witton, Birmingham.

We lived 10 minutes from Villa Park. This became a regular source of income during the football season, providing enough money to sustain the family for a week of basic food. More often than not I would make around 12 shillings which equates to 60p today, and my brothers would make the same.

In 1966, a Momentous occasion coincided with one of my car-minding ventures. The World Cup was held in England, and one of the matches took place at Aston Villa's ground between West Germany and Spain. On that remarkable day, through the generosity of the German supporters I earned a significant sum, £13.00, in old money, to be exact, a fortune at the time. One kind German supporter gave me a £5 note. I stood and cried; I could not believe his generosity. The joy I felt was amplified by Mom's happiness, knowing that we would have enough to feed the family for an entire month.

With a few shillings to spare, I relished the opportunity to treat my brothers, sister, and myself to sweets, something of a rarity to us.

I kept my earnings a secret from my Dad, because if he knew how much I had earned, he would have squandered most of it at the pub. The memories of that day remain etched in my heart.

As the autumn leaves painted the streets with hues of gold, a sense of anticipation would fill the air. November 5th was approaching, and with it, the excitement of Guy Fawkes Night (Bonfire night). For us, though, the days leading up to November the 5th, meant something more – it was an opportunity to channel our creativity into making a "guy" and getting out there on the streets on a mini-adventure that promised a few pennies in our pockets to give to our Mom.

Making the "guy" was an art that required imagination and resourcefulness.

Old clothes would be stitched together to form the body. Newspapers and rags meticulously shaped into a head. We would assemble our creation with pride, fashioning a makeshift hat or scarf for extra flair. Each "guy" had its own unique personality, a reflection of the collective imagination of us, children.

With our "guy" standing tall and our spirits high, we would venture to the local pubs, a mini army of aspiring entrepreneurs. The mission was simple: to politely ask passersby for a penny for the guy, please. We would share our story and explain our cause – to gather pennies for our "guy" so we could enjoy Bonfire Night in style.

Looking back, it was the camaraderie among us kids, the joy of displaying our guy to the world, and the interactions with kind-hearted individuals who shared a smile and a coin. Each encounter was a lesson in confidence and communication.

Guy-Fawking was not just about the money; it was a legacy of laughter and memories. It taught us that a bit of creativity and a sprinkle of courage could lead to unexpected rewards. The experience ingrained in us the value of initiative and the satisfaction of earning desperately needed money to provide food on the table.

As the calendar pages turned, Guy Fawkes Nights came and went, and our "guyfawking" adventures became stories we would recall with a chuckle. These tales serve as a reminder that even in the simplest childhood pursuits, there are lessons to be learned and memories to be cherished. It just goes to show that a little bit of creativity, determination, and a touch of mischief can transform ordinary moments into extraordinary memories that stand the test of time.

It is obvious that we were a wild bunch of outdoor enthusiasts. When the school holidays arrived in those sunny summer months, you could bet that we would be active from sunrise to sunset. We loved to play a game called Tracking. It involved two teams, one team finding the other, until the last member of the hiding team was caught. It could last for days at a time. The main venue was our local park.

Oh, the thrill of the hunt! We would have better luck finding buried treasure than locating our friends. That is what made it an adventure, we were so close, like peanut butter and jelly on a sandwich, always looking out for one another in the sprawling playground that was our neighbourhood.

Don't let our innocent escapades fool you. We were not just a gang of fun-loving explorers. No, we were a force to be reckoned with, a ragtag team of backyard defenders. There were these local troublemakers, led by a boy who always seemed to have his arm in plaster whom we named the Plaster of Paris kid, who thought it was their civic duty to pick on us. Always calling us names, maybe it was our superhero-like capes (a.k.a. bedsheet capes) that caught their attention, who knows?

Anyway, these showdowns with the neighbourhood "gangs" were not exactly Hollywood-style battles. Picture more like a mix of Karate moves with us flailing our arms like windmills. Yes, there were a few moments that got our heart rates up, but let us be real, we were not exactly training for the Olympics. Still, it was enough to make us consider becoming sprinters, just to be on the safe side.

The stories we collected during those days! From epic quests to neighbourhood showdowns, it was all a part of our unforgettable childhood saga. And through it all, we managed to create a bond that was stronger than any gang of local troublemakers. After all, what is a little fistfight compared to the lifelong friendships and stories that still make us laugh today.

As kids we loved to play football, our little gang of street football stars! We were like a pack of dogs chasing a "football". I am talking about that magical game were kicking a ball around felt like we were winning the World Cup.

Our street was our field of dreams, with its wide-open space and just a handful of cars that seemed to hibernate most of the time. Back then, the street was practically begging to be turned into our personal football stadium. We were like architects of play, transforming the cobble stones into a battleground of goals and glory.

At one end of the street, we had our "goalpost," which was someone's colourful jumper flapping in the breeze. It might not have been as fancy as those pro goalposts you see on TV, but it got the job done. And at the other end of the street, you had another makeshift goalpost, made from whatever we could find, like a discarded wooden box.

So, there we were, running back and forth like a bunch of speedy maniacs, chasing that ball like it was a golden ticket to Willy Wonka's chocolate factory. The sound of our obscure footwear screeching on the pavement was our version of the Champions League anthem, and our shouts and cheers could rival any stadium crowd.

You might be wondering, "What about the cars?" Let us just say they learned to avoid our soccer showdowns like the plague. If a car dared to wander into our playing field, it was met with a barrage of "STOP! Ball's out!" warnings that could wake up Sleeping Beauty. No car stood a chance against our enthusiastic cries of "OFFSIDE!" and "Wait, wait, I wasn't ready!"

Looking back, our street football matches were like our secret ticket to the old first division. We were our own heroes, Liverpool Everton, and Aston Villa players whose names created football magic in the most unexpected places. Who needed fancy stadiums and expensive equipment when we had our cobble stoned arena and trusty jumpers for goalposts? Those were the days, when we were football legends in our own neighbourhood, and our imaginations turned the street into our very own Wembley Stadium.

Chapter 6

Our Last Christmas at home with Mom and Dad

As children we looked forward to Christmas, and amidst the tinsel and twinkling lights of the festive season, our family's Christmas held a different kind of magic. The bittersweet charm of a Christmas that was not marked by abundance, but by the richness of gratitude and the warmth of togetherness.

Our home bore the simplicity of our circumstances. While other homes might have been adorned with lavish decorations, ours gleamed with something different – the light of unity and contentment. We had a Christmas tree, though modest in size, sparkling with homemade ornaments, each crafted with love and care by us.

On Christmas morning, the anticipation of excitement in the air was there for all to see. We gathered around our humble tree, where a few wrapped presents lay. While they may not have been as grand as those in storybooks, the value they held was immeasurable. Among the treasures, we found an apple and an orange, nestled among the wrapping paper. These simple fruits, symbols of abundance in their own right, were our Christmas presents.

Rather than disappointment, our hearts swelled with gratitude. The sight of those fruits represented more than their physical presence; they were tokens of love and sacrifice; we knew the lengths that Mom and Dad went to, to ensure that we had something special on this day. In their simplicity, they held the essence of what Christmas truly meant – giving, sharing, and cherishing the moments with loved ones.

Our Christmas dinner might not have been extravagant, but it was a banquet of togetherness. We gathered around the table, sharing stories and laughter, relishing the warmth that only family could provide. The aroma of a modest meal filled the air, and the taste of it was enhanced by the flavour of love in our hearts at the effort made by our Mom and Dad. The highlight of the day finished in the evening, where we all sang Christmas Carols.

Looking back, our poverty-stricken Christmases were not moments of lack; they were lessons in abundance. They taught us that true wealth lay in the intangible – in the bonds we shared, the love that flowed, and the gratitude that bloomed. Those simple presents, those humble feasts, were reminders that the value of a Moment was not determined by its extravagance, but by the heart and soul poured into it.

As the years passed, the memories of those Christmases have grown even more cherished. Those apples and oranges, yet simple gifts, hold a place of honour in my heart, a symbol of the love that transcends material wealth and the gratitude that forever enriches my life.

As I reflect on those precious moments now, I realise how truly fortunate we were to have each other. Our home may have been modest, our possessions few, but the love that bound us together was immeasurable. It was a love that sustained us through the challenges that lay ahead.

Little did I know then what trials awaited us as a family. The road ahead would be fraught with hardship, testing the strength of our bonds and the resilience of our spirits. Yet, in those fleeting moments of joy and togetherness, we laid the foundation for the unwavering support that would carry us through the darkest of times.

I am filled with gratitude for the memories we shared and the love that continues to sustain me. Though our time together was brief, the impact of those Christmases spent at home with Mom and Dad will live on in my heart forever. They are a reminder of the power of love in even the most challenging circumstances and the importance of cherishing every Moment we had together.

Chapter 7

Navigating Parenthood's Uncharted Waters

Each day brought a new lesson, each challenge an opportunity to prove my resilience.

I realised from an early age, that I had a deep empathy for my Mom's struggles and the hardship that the family faced. Witnessing her tears and desperation to feed the family left a lasting impact on me, igniting a desire to alleviate the suffering.

It was my love for my Mom that drove me to take on more responsibility. I felt a deep need to protect and support the family, even though I was just a young boy myself.

The sense of unfairness I felt stemmed from the realisation that I had to bear a burden that most young boys my age did not have to face, which influenced my outlook on life and my perception of what is "normal." It also meant making tough decisions, taking risks, and sacrificing my own desires and aspirations.

Nevertheless, the love and devotion I held for my Mom, propelled me forward, pushing me to persevere despite the challenges. The responsibility would shape my identity, resilience, and the profound sense of empathy I carried throughout my life.

Coping with Loss and Life-Altering Transitions

Loss is a companion on life's journey, a companion that sometimes sneaks up on us when we least expect it. It was as if the world held a mirror to my soul, reflecting the fragility of existence and the ephemeral nature of everything we hold dear. Losing loved ones felt like navigating a maze of emotions, where grief, anger, and acceptance intertwined like threads in a tapestry of sorrow.

As time passed, it became evident to me, even at such an early age, that my Mom's condition was deteriorating. Accompanying her to the hospital for specialist appointments, I witnessed her tears after one particular visit. Concerned, I questioned her, but she reassured me with a smile, urging me not to worry or share the news with my brothers and sister. The hospital visits became regular occurrences, resulting in me missing school for weeks on end to be with Mom at home.

Over the course of a year, Mom's treatment continued, and my dedication to caring for her grew stronger. However, the journey was not without hardship. One harrowing memory etched in my mind was Mom falling down a flight of stairs at the hospital. Despite my pleas for help, nobody intervened, leaving me feeling helpless as Mom struggled to her feet, enduring excruciating pain. The arduous journey home on that day, on multiple buses further amplified our distress.

The prolonged nature of Mom's treatment for cancer meant she had to spend extended periods in hospital, resulting in her absence from us. These were incredibly trying times for my brothers, sister, and me. As her cancer spread to other parts of her body, my Mom experienced severe pain, necessitating heavy sedation and long hours in bed. I was, overcome with sadness, and often I would lie beside her during the day. I experienced a feeling of emptiness.

In a heart-wrenching Moment, just days before Mom's passing, Mom held my hand and candidly shared the gravity of her condition. Torn apart by the thought of losing her, I could not contain myself. Despite my awareness of her illness, hearing her acknowledge the possibility of her imminent departure was devastating.

On that never forgotten day, as I lay down on the bed with her, she implored me to be strong and to promise her that I would take care of my brothers and sister, a pledge I wholeheartedly made. Not realising at such an early age how that one Moment would impact my life for ever.

As a young child, I had not fully grasped the gravity of Mom's illness initially. However, there had been subtle signs and growing concerns within the family. I did notice her increasing weakness, and the strain on us all as we cared for her.

Seeing my Mom's pain and suffering, even at an early age, I felt a deep concern for her well-being.

I felt moments of vulnerability and fear in Mom, which had an impact on me.

Growing up in a large family, as I did, often necessitates cooperation and support among siblings. In many families, older siblings naturally take on roles as caregivers and protectors, especially when parents face challenges. It becomes a part of the family dynamic.

In my case, it seems that a combination of factors, such as empathy, family dynamics, and my Mom's trust, contributed to my willingness to step forward and care for my brothers and sister. This sense of responsibility likely became a defining aspect of my character and played a significant role in my life journey.

This period in my life was an extreme and premature introduction to the challenges and responsibilities that lay ahead. It forced me to grow up quickly and make decisions beyond my years.

Chapter 8

Mom's Passing

I hold a vivid recollection of the day preceding my mother's passing. It is still in my memory as if it happened only yesterday. She came downstairs, her presence radiating a sense of normality and strength despite the impending struggle she faced.

Fully dressed and composed, she moved among us as though the weight of her condition had been momentarily lifted. I can still feel the warmth of her embrace as she gathered each one of us in her arms, showering us with love and affection that felt like a soothing balm for our collective worries.

What remains imprinted in my mind is her smile. It was a genuine expression of joy that belied the impending storm. Her cheeks bore a rosy hue, a result of the lipstick she had applied with care. It was her way of concealing the paleness that had taken hold of her complexion. The contrast between the vibrant rosiness of her cheeks and the reality of her underlying condition created an image that encapsulated her strength and the lengths to which she went to shield us from her pain.

In that Moment, her smile radiated amongst all of us, it was a symbol of her love and resilience. It was a reminder that she found the strength to give us a final memory of her warmth and love. It is a memory I hold close, a picture that shows a Moment that I will never forget, her spirit and the depth of the love she had for us children.

On May 31, 1967, Mom succumbed to cancer, leaving a void that would forever be felt by the family. The subsequent weeks were a blur, with unfamiliar faces coming and going to look after us. What was evident was the despair shown by Dad, you could see he was still deeply in love with Mom, he was shattered by her loss. His inconsolable grief manifested in incessant drinking and days spent bedridden. Only my older brother was allowed in Dad's room, witnessing the depths of his anguish.

Coping with the loss of Mom and the prospect of him having to raise eight children alone was emotionally devastating for him. His grief, sadness, and feelings of being overwhelmed consumed him as he realised the enormity of the task ahead.

The impact on his well-being was there for all to see, the stress and pressure of single-handedly raising eight children had a profound impact on his physical and mental well-being.

In the shadow of my Mom's passing, a different kind of transformation unfolded – one that highlighted the fragility of the human spirit in the face of loss - my Dad, a man of towering strength who found himself navigating the depths of grief, and the remarkable journey that emerged from his pain.

At six feet tall, he exuded a confidence that inspired admiration. His powerful presence could fill a room, and his gentle heart endeared him to all who knew him.

The day my Mom left this world, a seismic shift occurred within our family. For my Dad, the loss was not just an emotional void; it was a cataclysm that evaluated the very foundation of his being. The woman he had loved, laughed with, and shared life's joys and sorrows was suddenly gone. In her absence, the world he had known crumbled.

In the months that followed, the pain etched across my Dad's face was a mirror to the turmoil within. His physical transformation was stark – the robust figure that had been a pillar of strength seemed to wither away before our eyes. The broad shoulders that had carried our family now bore the weight of sorrow.

My father's metamorphosis was a testament to the depth of his love and the gravity of his loss. The clothes that once fitted snugly now hung loose, a reflection of the emptiness that had taken residence within.

Tragedy struck again just nine months after Mom's passing. Dad, at the tender age of 39, succumbed to the relentless grasp of tuberculosis. The pain of losing him so soon after Mom created a heartrending double loss that cast a deep shadow over our family. The once-familiar rhythms of our lives were shattered, replaced by the harsh discord of grief and confusion.

In the wake of Dad's departure, the days that followed were clouded with confusion. The stark reality of a life without both parents was unbearable.

We were thrust into uncertainty, grappling with the harsh truth that the contagious illness that claimed Dad had inevitably touched our lives. The fear and uncertainty that gripped us became a formidable adversary, and the once-stable ground beneath our feet felt like shifting sands.

The heartbreak intensified as circumstances prevented me from attending Dad's funeral. The very act of bidding my final goodbyes, a ritual that serves as a poignant closure, was denied to me. The pain of being kept away from that sacred Moment left a void, a sense of unresolved closure that cast a long, haunting shadow over me. The inability to say a proper goodbye became a burden that echoed through the corridors of my grief-stricken heart.

The disease that had taken Dad so young had found its way into my fragile body, through living with conditions at home that were cold and damp and seeing to Dad every day as he lay dying. I could feel it tightening with each passing day. The coughs that once echoed with youthful exuberance now carried the weight of an ominous secret, and the vibrancy of my youth dimmed under the weight of fatigue and despair.

Our home, once a sanctuary of warmth and laughter, transformed into a place shrouded in cold and dampness. The very elements that should have provided comfort now became conduits for the relentless progression of the disease. The chilling atmosphere seemed to echo the sombre tones of our grief, as if the very walls mourned the loss of the vibrant lives that once filled our humble home.

As the days passed, the insidious grip of the disease tightened its hold on my fragile body. Life had thrust me into a silent battleground where the consequences of love, care, and unavoidable circumstances converged. The once-innocent moments became fraught with the complexity of silent struggles, and the fragility of my body bore witness to the silent intrusion of a disease that had stealthily crept into the fabric of our lives. The realisation dawned that the battle against both seen and unseen adversaries had become an integral part of my journey through the labyrinth of grief and resilience.

During the 1960s in the UK, tuberculosis cast a pervasive shadow, earning its grim reputation as a silent and ruthless killer. The infectious disease, once considered a formidable adversary in the battle for public health, had not yet been fully tamed by medical advancements. It lurked in the shadows, taking a toll on families and communities, leaving an indelible mark on the landscape of healthcare during that era.

Tuberculosis, commonly known as TB, was a looming threat that haunted households across the United Kingdom in the 1960s. Its presence was felt in the crowded urban centres and the quieter rural landscapes alike, creating an atmosphere of unease. The spectre of the disease lingered in the minds of the populace, a constant reminder of the fragility of life and the unpredictable nature of health in an era where medical breakthroughs were still on the horizon.

Beyond its physical toll, tuberculosis brought with it a heavy burden of stigma and fear. The infected were often shunned, and communities lived in anxiety about the potential outbreak of the disease. TB was not merely a medical challenge; it was a major social concern that gripped the collective consciousness, influencing daily decisions and altering the social fabric of communities.

The battle against tuberculosis was waged with limited medical resources. The healthcare infrastructure in the UK at the time grappled with the enormity of the challenge, and the tools available for diagnosis, treatment, and prevention were not as advanced as those we have today. The medical community faced an uphill struggle to curb the spread of TB and provide effective care to those afflicted by the disease.

The threat of tuberculosis prompted public health campaigns aimed at raising awareness and encouraging preventative measures. Communities were educated about the importance of hygiene, proper ventilation, and early detection. These campaigns sought to empower individuals with the knowledge needed to protect themselves and their loved ones from the insidious reach of tuberculosis.

Families like mine found themselves navigating the harsh impact of tuberculosis firsthand. The fear of contagion, coupled with the challenges of limited medical resources, created an environment where every cough, every Moment of fatigue, was viewed through the lens of potential infection. The spectre of TB, with its silent and unpredictable nature, transformed everyday life into a delicate dance with an unseen adversary.

Beyond the physical toll, tuberculosis exacted a heavy emotional toll on families. The uncertainty surrounding its prognosis, coupled with the societal stigma, intensified the already challenging landscape of grief. Families faced not only the loss of loved ones but also the pervasive anxiety that accompanied the era's struggles with infectious diseases.

As the years unfolded, medical advancements gradually transformed the landscape of tuberculosis treatment. Antibiotics and improved diagnostic tools emerged, leading to a more effective response to TB. The once-feared killer began to lose its grip, marking a turning point in the battle against this formidable disease.

The collective efforts to overcome the challenges posed by TB laid the groundwork for a future where medical science would triumph over what was once an insurmountable adversary, bringing hope to future generations.

Chapter 9

Living with Tuberculosis

As I stepped into the stark confines of East Birmingham Hospital, a place where countless souls had fought their own battles against this merciless disease, a sense of trepidation mingled with a flicker of hope. The walls were sterile, the air heavy with the scent of antiseptics, and the whispers of prayers and fragmented dreams lingered in the corridors. At that point I had no idea of how seriously ill I was.

Days blurred into weeks, weeks into months, as I embarked on a gruelling regimen of treatments designed to combat the relentless bacteria ravaging my body. Bed rest became my companion, and I would be put outside the ward in my bed for hours every day, as the fresh air was part of the healing process.

Within the confines of that sterile environment, I discovered an inner strength that defied the very essence of my illness. I will never forget the kindness of the nursing staff, one in particular, (Nurse Dyson) who looked after "The Ranford Ward". She went that extra mile to ensure that everyone got the best treatment. Her sense of humour resonated around the ward, she cared about her patients.

I remember waking one morning to see that there was someone new in the ward. His name as I found out was Mohamed, whose bed was adjacent to mine. He embodied resilience in its purest form. His body bore the visible scars of this relentless disease, yet his spirit remained unyielding, unbroken. We built up a friendship over time and he became my friend.

During my time in hospital, I did not receive any visitors, and I was always puzzled by that. It made me wonder why people did not come to see me. However, something remarkable happened - Mohammed's family, who visited him daily, extended their kindness to me. They would often bring me fruit to eat and sweets, a gesture that touched me deeply.

Their generosity and compassion never failed to astound me. It is a powerful reminder of how we sometimes underestimate the goodness that exists within our fellow human beings. In a situation where I felt alone and overlooked, their simple acts of kindness brought a sense of warmth and connection. Their visits, offering not just physical gifts but also a sense of caring and companionship, made a significant impact on my perspective.

This experience taught me that even in moments of solitude, a small act of kindness has the power to bridge gaps, create bonds, and restore our faith in humanity. It is a lesson that I have carried with me, as a reminder to always extend kindness to others and to be open to the unexpected ways in which it can touch our lives.

Over the next six months, we navigated the treacherous waters of recovery, sharing stories of how our lives beyond the confines of the sanatorium walls would work out, I knew that I faced an uncertain future having no choice but to be sent to an orphanage. We dreamed of the lives we would lead once we emerged victorious, and we found strength in each other's unwavering determination to overcome the odds stacked against us.

As I lay in my bed, my body wracked by bouts of coughing, I turned my attention to the written word. Books became my companions, transporting me to distant lands and immersing me in the tales of characters who fought their own battles. It was through these pages that I discovered the power of imagination, a force that transcended the boundaries of my physical limitations.

As time wore on, the pendulum of my health swung with uncertainty. There were moments of despair when the spectre of death loomed ominously. But within me, a voice whispered, urging me to embrace the strength that lay dormant within me. To this day I believe it was my Mom watching over me, willing me to come through.

During my stay in hospital I underwent intense treatment, including daily injections and oral medication. The kind nurses, regular meals, and access to education through the hospital school offered respite from the hardships I had known.

The day approached for my discharge, and a real sense of anxiety overwhelmed me, as I faced an uncertain future at the orphanage. Emotionally distraught, I pleaded with the nurses, expressing my fear and reluctance to be sent there. The impending transition represented yet another life-altering Moment for me.

Finally, the day arrived when I was deemed fit to leave the confines of the sanatorium, my lungs once again filled with the breath of life. Mohammed, too, emerged triumphant just a few weeks before me, his spirit unwavering in the face of adversity.

The battle against tuberculosis had shaped me in ways I could never have foreseen. It taught me the value of life, the fragility of existence, and how humans are resilient. The scars on my lungs became a reminder of the strength that flowed through my veins, the indomitable spirit that refused to be extinguished. I entered the new lease on life that tuberculosis afforded me. I recount the triumphs and setbacks, the joyous moments and heart-wrenching losses that would define my journey. Through it all, the memory of Mohammed's strength and desire to live would stay with me for ever.

⸻◈⸻

Chapter 10

The Orphanage: Navigating the Unseen Realms of Childhood

The orphanage was a door I never expected to open, a threshold that led to a world I had never imagined. As a child, it was like stepping into a new reality, where rules and routines differed from what I had known. It was a place that carried a weight of uncertainty and unfamiliarity, yet it was also a place that offered refuge.

It was a chapter of my childhood that imprinted itself on my soul, shaping my understanding of community, and the strength that emerges from shared hardships.

Life inside the Orphanage

The vivid memory of driving down what seemed an exceptionally long road and arriving at the orphanage gates left me with a powerful vision, one that I would never forget.

The impact of those images reflects the significance of the Moment and the emotions associated with it.

As I approached the gates, my eyes were drawn to an imposing figure standing before me. A woman of great stature. Who would be someone that would become a nightmare to me during my stay.

The woman's commanding presence captured my attention immediately.

Her towering figure filled the space around her, radiating a sense of awe and respect. The choice of a black robe added a touch of gravitas to her appearance.

The mysterious veil! It was like a black curtain, hiding past secrets.

There I stood, face to veil, ready to embark on an adventure of mystery and discovery.

The contrasting colours evoked a sense of duality, reflecting both the strictness and care that often coexist in such environments. Having encountered a figure of such stature and appearance on my arrival left me with an impression, particularly as it was my first meeting with someone who would become a significant part of my life in the orphanage.

The iron gates to the orphanage themselves evoked feelings of separation and confinement, as they marked the entrance to an unfamiliar environment that would become my world for the next 5 years. In the depths of my memory, that place that shaped the very core of my being - an orphanage that became my home, should have been my sanctuary.

The main orphanage building itself was nestled away, as though deliberate, from the prying eyes of outsiders. It stood as a refuge for countless souls, each with their own stories of abandonment and longing. The structure with weathered stone walls and a roof that seemed to sag under the weight of decades, held within its embrace a tapestry of lives intertwined. The halls echoed with the pitter-patter of tiny feet, the laughter of children yearning for love, and the sighs of priests and nuns burdened with the weight of responsibility.

For me, it was supposed to be sanctuary of fleeting stability, a haven in a world fraught with uncertainty. How I was let down by my experiences at the hands of those who should have been protecting me.

In those shared spaces, I formed a family of misfits bound by circumstance.

The faces of my fellow orphans, etched with the hardships they had endured, became the backdrop of part of my childhood.

From the precocious Annie with her fiery spirit to timid little James, who clung to his tattered stuffed bear, and the vision of Oliver Twist asking for more, we each carried within us a longing for stability and a yearning for connection.

I spent the first 6 months recovering from the illness that nearly killed me. As time went by, I was slowly introduced to the regular routine of everyday life. Within the orphanage there appeared to be a rhythmic routine, providing a semblance of structure in a world that seemed intent on chaos. Up every day at the crack of dawn, greeted by the melodic chimes of the chapel bell. Calling the nuns for 5 am mass.

As we sat, bleary-eyed but hopeful, as altar boys, we had to recite prayers, seeking peace in the divine as we embarked on another day.

The days were long and arduous, packed with detailed work, such as cleaning, in between school. My chores included waxing, and polishing the dormitories, and cleaning floors on my hands and knees in the huge wash lavatories. I was not very strong, my body still recovering from the disease that I had almost succumbed to months earlier. It used to take me longer than the other children, and I would be punished for being too slow by missing out on playtime.

The one thing that I really loved was being at school, it was respite for me from the daily routine.

Education was a light, a beacon of possibility, was a privilege I cherished.

Our classroom, adorned with worn-out textbooks and chalk-dusted blackboards, became a gateway to a world beyond the orphanage walls. Under the patient guidance of dedicated teachers, I learned to navigate the curriculum and dream of a future that was beyond my circumstances. My dread was the school holidays and what that entailed, extra work. In the early summer months of me being there I was lucky to be asked to help on the farm a few days a week. It was such a refreshing change I was out in the fresh air, working with the cows.

That first summer, unexpectedly 4 of the Conway family children were chosen to go and spend that first summer in a Children Respite Centre outside Oslo, in Norway.

The news that social services had arranged for us to spend the main summer months at an international children's rehabilitation centre in Oslo, brought a glimmer of hope amidst the challenging circumstances we were facing.

This opportunity offered a chance for recovery and respite from the harsh realities of our lives.

The purpose of the trip was to aid the recovery from our illness.

The journey to Oslo held the promise of medical care, fresh mountain air, and a conducive environment for recuperation. The orphanage saw this as a critical step in ensuring our health and well-being.

The prospect of spending an entire summer in Norway was an adventure. It meant a break from the crowded orphanage and a chance to explore a new country. Norway's natural beauty, with its fjords, forests, and clean air, was a stark contrast to the urban environment we had become accustomed to.

At the rehabilitation centre, we received one to one specialist medical care.

This included regular check-ups, medication, and a regime designed to strengthen our immune systems and aid in our recovery. The focus was on ensuring that our health improved during the stay.

While the centre offered physical healing, it also had emotional significance. This trip provided a sense of normality from the challenges that we faced daily. It was a chance to be children again, to play, explore, and form positive memories. There were other children there whom we built up relationships with beyond our stay. Every child that was there had life threatening illnesses and unfortunately during the trip some of them lost their fight for life.

The trip represented a unique opportunity for us all. It was not only a crucial step in our physical recovery but also a chance to experience a different environment and find moments of joy and healing amidst the challenges we had faced. This experience left a lasting memory on all of us, shaping our perspective on life and the world.

Returning from our journey my heart was filled with a mix of emotions, like a ship navigating uncharted waters. As we crossed the choppy North Sea from Kristiansand to Newcastle to the threshold of familiar shores, the memories of that summer echoed in the chambers of my mind.

The rugged beauty of Norway's fjords and the crisp, pure air had left an indelible mark on my soul. The laughter of my brothers and sister, the kindness of the people there, and the friendships forged with children from distant lands lingered like stars in a midnight sky.

But as the Norwegian landscape faded from view, a new chapter began, one where the lessons of resilience and hope, learned on that distant shore, would guide me through life's tumultuous seas. I carried with me the strength, the love of family that had sustained us, and the belief that even in the darkest of storms, there was a light to guide us home.

With each passing year, I have come to understand that life is a journey filled with both triumphs and tribulations. And as I stand on the precipice of tomorrow, I do so with a heart filled not only with the worry of the unknown but also with the hope that, like the ship returning to port, my voyage will be guided by the stars of resilience, love, and the enduring human spirit.

With gratitude for the past and hope for the future, I set sail into the horizon, ready to embrace the adventures that awaited me. The journey continues, and so does the story.

⊷⊷⊱❬❪◇❫❭⊰⊶⊶

Chapter 11

Enduring the Pain of Physical and Mental Abuse

Yet, despite the fleeting moments of joy and the loving guidance of a few nuns who embraced their roles as surrogate parents, a palpable sense of longing permeated the air.

My anger to the unpunished perpetrators who enabled a systematic program of both physical and sexual abuse to continue within this so-called safe orphanage will be one that I could not let go. Not only the priests, but also the nuns.

Like one parent that has full knowledge that the other parent is abusing a child, it is not acceptable to "turn a blind eye" to the situation.

I was one of many altar boys and would serve mass in the chapel most days. I remember the day as if it was yesterday the first time I was faced with the predator, the priest who was about to befriend me and subsequently sexually abuse me for more than 4 years.

I was putting out the candles after mass, I could feel that someone was looking at me. He started to talk to me. I had never seen this person before. At first, I thought he was nice, he was asking me if I had settled in, and if I was starting to feel better. He said to me that he wanted me to think of him as someone that I could talk to if I had any worries, and that he would make sure that I was not bullied. In the school holidays there were several visiting priests that would spend their holiday at the homes. My abuser came from a parish in Stratford-upon-Avon and he would appear every school holiday. I would say, but could not be 100% sure, that he was in his sixties. During the holidays he would ask the nuns to send me up to his room so that he could talk to me.

When I entered his room he locked the door, I asked him not to, but he still locked it.

This was the first time I was taken into his room. He sat on the edge of the bed. If I described the room because I can still see what was in it, there was a single bed, a bedside table with a crucifix on the wall, and a single wardrobe. The room had a smell of incense. The smell lives with me today and returns to me as a nightmare every time I go into a church.

He asked me to come and sit next to him on the bed. He said, "Do not be frightened, I just want to talk to you and find out more about you." He put his arm around my shoulders and asked me to lie down on the bed next to him.

I could feel him next to me, he had his clothes on, and there was a smell coming off him that I can still smell today. It was semen. I didn't know what it was back then. He started making a funny grunting noise and he was shaking, he grabbed my hand and put it on his private parts and pressed up against me. He then said, "Just lie with me for a few minutes." Those few minutes seemed like hours, and I started getting to my feet, and he said for me not to say anything to anyone. Little did I know at the time that was the start of horrific events that would involve explicit sexual penetration, and oral activities, and I could do nothing about it.

I built up the courage and told one of the nuns whom I thought I could confide in. That was a huge mistake for me. She went straight to the Mother Superior and said that I was making up stories about father X. As a result, I was beaten with a leather strap until I could not stand up, by the Mother Superior, and I had carbolic soap thrust into my mouth, and I was beaten with a wet towel whilst naked on the floor of the wash lavatory by another nun. I was ordered to confession to tell the priest that I was lying about what had happened to me. I thought that confession allowed us to hold ourselves accountable for lies and we should ask God for true forgiveness. I had not done anything wrong; I was not lying so why did I need to confess? I was confused and was trying to tell the priest what had happened to me. The priest pulled back the black shade of the confessional box and told me to wait for him, until he had finished hearing other confessions.

What happened afterwards was a vendetta against me. This was the start of me being isolated, detached, lonely, secluded. I believed that a priest taking confessions was supposed to be a representative of God, and whatever he hears should have been sacred. I felt trapped with nowhere to go, I was devastated. I was crying for my Mom to help me. As the weeks went by, I was getting incredibly low in mood, because I could not tell anyone what was happening to me. My mental state was getting worse, and I became very withdrawn. At first, I tried everything to stop it, even running away, but it did not stop my dread that was to last for years, and I could do nothing about it. The abuse continued until I left the orphanage. I pleaded with the nuns, expressing my fear and pain, but it fell on deaf ears.

It was yet another life-altering Moment filled with uncertainty.

The orphanage, though a sanctuary, held within it the bittersweet reminder of what we had lost. Birthdays celebrated without my parents' warm embrace; milestones marked without loved ones to cheer us on - these were the invisible scars etched upon our souls of the constant sexual abuse that permeated through the institution. Yet, it was within these scars that resilience was born, the determination to carve out a life of purpose and meaning.

As I reflect upon my time in the orphanage, the memories intertwine like threads in a tapestry. The laughter and tears, my fear, the unspoken friendship, and the support of a few, became the foundation upon which I would build my life.

Chapter 12

Change of Mentality

As the months went by, I was asked if I wanted to work in the kitchen, instead of scrubbing floors and waxing the dormitories. I was very weak and was still recovering from my illness. I thought it might be better for me to work in a less labour intensive environment. I found out that the role of kitchen boy was instigated by my abuser.

At first, I was upset, and I refused to do it, but then I realised that I might be able to change one or two things. For example, the quality of the food that was being produced, was so unpalatable. To give an example, the potatoes would still have their eyes sticking out of them, and they were starting to rot. The bread would have mold growing on it. The breakfast cereal was out of date, and the milk was straight from the cow, with lumps in it. I thought if I could even change the basic preparation processes, by taking out the eyes of the potatoes and keeping the bread in tins, and straining the milk, then the children would start to look forward to meals. I believed that I could make a significant improvement. So, I decided to embrace this opportunity to make a positive impact.

The food being given to us daily would consist of a small bowl of cereal for breakfast, and if we were not at school, we would have soup and bread, and in the evening, a cup of either milk or gruel.

I took it upon myself to address the issues, such as the inferior quality of ingredients and the unsanitary conditions. I was kidding myself that it would not take me long to make changes, but it wasn't easy as there was a hierarchy in place, where I was bottom of the list when I first went in, but as time went by, I found myself at the top of the hierarchical system, as head kitchen boy. It meant that I could start to win over the nun who oversaw the kitchen and start to slowly introduce changes.

At first it was difficult to get to even talk to her because there were always other nuns around, but my determination to create meals that were not only nourishing but also appealing was my priority.

It was like a parallel universe because the food that was prepared and given to the nuns and priest was of a five-star quality, the children had what was left over.

The Moment that I first entered the kitchen was overwhelming and a real surprise, the huge space took my breath away. The large machines, and the bustling atmosphere that accompanied the preparation of food on a larger scale, was something that I had never seen before. I started to see why the children were strictly prohibited from entering the kitchen. In total there were at least 20 working in there, some were children, but the majority were nuns.

The challenges that I was about to face as I familiarised myself with the kitchen's equipment and processes were daunting for me. It was a learning curve. I had to understand and learn quickly how to operate the cooking ranges and vegetable peeling machines, as part of my job at the time was preparation.

We were catering for over 500 children, nuns, and priests.

My main mission was to start to improve the quality of the food being served as soon as I was able.

When I first started work the conditions that I observed came as no surprise, there were bags of rotting potatoes, stacked in piles in a room adjacent to the kitchen. So, I worked tirelessly to prepare the ingredients, implement proper storage techniques, and enhance the overall standards of the meals. As I reflect on my personal fulfilment and satisfaction from the success of making a few basic changes to how to prepare food, it was clearly evident on the smiles on those faces as the ultimate reward for my hard work.

One of the biggest hurdles that I was facing was how to stop the bullying of the smaller children by the senior boys and girls.

The pervasive bullying of smaller children by senior boys and girls was yet another dark shadow cast over the atmosphere of the home. Witnessing the fear and oppression that these younger children endured at the hands of their older peers stirred a fire within me, igniting a fierce determination to put an end to this cycle of abuse and restore a sense of safety and dignity to all who called the home their refuge.

Recognising that the issue of bullying was not unique to our home, but rather a widespread phenomenon that plagued many institutions, I knew that decisive action was needed to address it head-on. The smaller children, coerced into submission by the older ones, were forced to surrender their meals and perform menial tasks under threat of violence and punishment. It was a heartbreaking reality that could not be allowed to continue.

I was on a mission to confront the perpetrators of this injustice and negotiate a truce that would bring an end to the reign of terror. It was a daunting task, fraught with challenges and uncertainties, but I was undeterred in my commitment to achieving peace for all who resided within the walls of the home.

Crafting a plan with meticulous care, I set out to meet with the individuals responsible for the bullying, offering them a proposition that would exchange their control for cooperation and mutual respect. It was a delicate balance of diplomacy and determination, as I sought to appeal to their sense of reason and humanity while standing firm in my resolve to protect the rights and well-being of the smaller children.

It took me months of tireless effort and persistent negotiation, but eventually, my message began to penetrate the walls of resistance that had been erected by years of oppression and fear. The promise of better-quality food and increased portions served as a powerful incentive for cooperation, while my unwavering commitment to enforcing consequences for any acts of violence or intimidation lent credibility to my efforts.

Slowly but surely, the tide began to turn, and the once dominant culture of bullying began to crumble beneath the weight of newfound cooperation and understanding. With each passing day, instances of violence and intimidation grew increasingly rare.

It was a victory not just for the smaller children who had long suffered under the tyranny of their older peers, but for the collective spirit of the home as a whole.

As I reflect on those challenging days, I am reminded of the profound truth that peace is not simply the absence of conflict, but rather the presence of justice and understanding. Through negotiation and perseverance, we were able to achieve a semblance of peace within the walls of our home, proving that even in the darkest of times, the light of hope and humanity can shine through.

The challenges that arose from working in a restricted area:

One of my main challenges was, how I navigated the locked doors and the secrecy surrounding the kitchen. To my amazement I discovered that the kitchen had a number of locked pantries that stored all of the food including biscuits, chocolate, and other ingredients, which were used in the preparation of the banquets that were enjoyed daily by the nuns and priests. While the children under their care had leftovers. Over time I was given access to those pantries and boy! Did the children enjoy the fruits of my discovery!! On occasions there were close calls or moments when I had to be cautious to avoid being caught. I wanted to share some of those luxuries with the children, and I am not proud of what I did to make that happen but smiles on faces was enough for me. I did go to confession and told the priest. It's funny that no one confronted me over it.

Being able to make these small adjustments in process instilled confidence in my ability to create change, and further fuelled my determination to succeed in all aspects of my life. Those early memories hold a certain weight and significance because they represent a pivotal Moment of change and adaptation. They serve as reminders of the journey that I had taken and the experiences that have shaped me into the person I am today.

As my parents were part of the Irish community, they often used to attend their local social club in Small Heath Birmingham. What we didn't know at the time was that in the background members of the club would organise raffles and events in aid of the Conway family, and every Thursday evening we would get a visit from club members with huge bags of sweets that we were happy to share with all of the children in the orphanage. We really looked forward to their visits.

As my time at the orphanage drew to a close, a mix of emotions flooded my heart. Leaving behind the only home I had known for years stirred feelings of apprehension. The familiar routines, faces, had become a part of my identity, yet I also felt a growing sense of excitement and anticipation for the journey ahead.

Walking out of the orphanage gates, I carried with me feelings of anger at the perpetrators who will continue their abuse of other innocent children. I will remember the moments of connection shared with fellow residents and the few special nuns. Despite the challenges and hardships I had faced within those walls, the orphanage had also been a place of learning.

Stepping into the unknown, I was filled with a sense of determination to carve out a new path for myself, to seek opportunities. While uncertainty lay ahead, I held onto the hope that the next chapter of my life would bring new adventures, friendships, and possibilities.

Chapter 13

A Journey of Self-Discovery: Leaving the Orphanage

Leaving the orphanage was like standing at a crossroads, facing the intersection of what had been and what could be. The familiar walls that had sheltered me were now a backdrop to a new chapter, one that held both excitement and uncertainty. It was a Moment that signalled the end of an era and the beginning of a journey towards self-discovery. It was time to emerge as a transformed butterfly, ready to embrace my new challenge.

I was 15 years old when I was finally allowed to leave the orphanage that had been my home for 5 years. It was a mixture of relief, fear, and uncertainty that filled my heart as I packed my meagre belongings into a small bag. Leaving behind the familiar faces and routines of the orphanage was both liberating and daunting. I was also upset about leaving behind my youngest two brothers, and my sister, wondering if I would see them again, but holding onto the hope of a reunion as soon as I could. The thought of seeing them again further fuelled my determination to succeed. I was imagining the joyous embrace and the prospect of being reunited with them once again out of this awful institution.

As I walked out of those familiar gates, I could not help but reflect on the journey that had brought me to this Moment. Growing up without the presence of my parents had shaped me in ways I could not fully comprehend.

Leaving the orphanage meant stepping into a world that was unfamiliar and unforgiving. I had to face the harsh realities of life head-on, in the outside world.

Armed with nothing but £6 in my pocket, and my determination to create a better future for myself, there were no safety nets or handouts waiting for me. The harsh reality was it was up to me to navigate the challenges that lay ahead.

After leaving the orphanage I was sent temporarily to a halfway house, with 4 other boys and my twin brother. It should have been a stepping-stone towards independence and stability, but instead, it became a challenging and uncomfortable experience.

"The Masters" as they were known, were all male and they were intimidating. There were stories of abuse that circulated the place, and I felt extremely uncomfortable and uneasy around them. I had made up my mind that I did not want to be there to suffer any more abuse. I was determined to leave that institutional life behind me. The decision not to stay left me facing the harsh reality of homelessness, a situation filled with uncertainty and vulnerability. That decision not to stay thrust me into the unknown, unsure of where to turn or how to find stability. The decision that I made to leave was life changing for me. But I did not want to be facing more abuse.

I had been in this situation many times, and I was determined that no one would ever force me to do anything that I did not want to do. Ever again!

With limited resources, the road ahead seemed arduous. However, the same grit and determination that had carried me through challenging times in the past fuelled my determination to succeed. Sleeping rough on the streets in the 1970s was a traumatic ordeal. The nights were eternally long, filled with bone-chilling cold and a gnawing hunger that seemed insatiable. The absence of human connection weighed heavily on my spirit, and I often found myself yearning for the familiar comfort of a home and the warmth of my loved ones.

Each day brought a new wave of fear and vulnerability. I felt like a shadow in a world bustling with people, yet unable to see me. I navigated the urban landscape of the Birmingham suburbs with caution, constantly on guard against the dangers that lurked in the shadows. The threat of violence, theft, and exploitation loomed, forcing me to be aware of my surroundings and ever ready to protect myself.

Meeting basic survival needs became an all-consuming task. Food was a luxury I could not afford, and I resorted to scavenging for scraps or relying on the goodwill of strangers.

My nights were the worst, I spent time seeking refuge in a disused electrical box at Witton railway station Birmingham, tucked away in forgotten corners or seeking shelter in abandoned buildings, where the biting November cold seemed to seep through every crack and crevice. I was alone, tired and so hungry.

I had a mental map of every nook and cranny that offered a chance of a warm meal and/ or a clean shirt. It was like being part of a secret society, except instead of secret handshakes, I relied on the kindness of local neighbours and charities.

Speaking of charities, I want to give a round of applause to the Boot Night Shelter in Digbeth, Birmingham. Those people were like the real-life versions of guardian angels, often providing warm meals and clean clothes.

It was not all doom and gloom – there were moments of triumph in discovering a hidden stash of baked beans or finding a pair of socks that matched. Who knew that hardship could also be a crash course in urban exploration and the fine art of scavenger hunting? If anything, those tough times taught me that when life throws bad apples at you, you can make a surprisingly good makeshift apple pie.

I even resorted to being picked up by the police on many occasions for sleeping in doorways (there were Draconian "Vagrancy laws" in 1970s in England) and I would risk being charged but if it meant a warm cell overnight and breakfast in the morning, I would gratefully take that.

The Vagrancy Act was initially intended to deal with injured ex-serviceman who had become homeless after the Napoleonic Wars. Their crime after serving their country? Endeavouring by the exposure of wounds or deformities to obtain or gather alms or procure charitable contributions of any nature or kind, under any false or fraudulent pretence according to the act. This means ex-soldiers were begging and the Act was brought in to stop it.

The Vagrancy Act also aimed to punish "every person wandering abroad and lodging in any barn or outhouse, or in any deserted or unoccupied building, or in the open air, or under a tent, or in any cart or waggon," namely transient people, typically from Scotland or Ireland, who were considered undesirable. The Act also represented a threat to

Gypsy, traveller, and Roma communities. Thank God the Act was repealed by law in April 2022.

There were times that I was offered shelter by individuals who would hang around the all-night cafes looking for vulnerable young prey. Little did I know at the time that I was that young prey! I remember that I nearly succumbed to such an individual. It was in December, and it was freezing cold outside, and I was at my lowest point. I went into a café called the Towrope on Broad Street Birmingham, just to keep warm. I had no money, and I was cold, tired and hungry. I was approached by a man who was no older than 30. He started talking to me and he offered to buy me a cup of tea and said that he had a spare room in his house and that I could sleep there. He was extremely nice to me, and I was desperate to get some sleep, so I said that I would go with him. I felt a real sense of unease as we approached his house which was a 10 minute walk from the Café. However, I was so cold, hungry and tired.

At first things seemed to be ok, and I was shown the room, it was clean and warm and before I knew it, I had fallen asleep on top of the bed. I was woken in a startle by this man putting his hand down my trousers. I panicked and started to scream and shout for him to get off me. Eventually I forced him off and I managed to get out of the house and run with every scrap of energy I had, to the safety of the streets.

Everything that I had experienced in the orphanage started to come back to me with a real fear of me being in danger again, the thought that this individual could have killed me was so frightening. I was only 15 years of age and alone. It was the one and only time that it happened to me, that I was so lucky that December night.

There were also other instances when I was exposed to individuals with malicious intentions. The encounter I have described with the man who offered me shelter but turned out to be a threat was deeply distressing. It highlights the vulnerability and dangers faced by those in desperate situations. My instincts that night to fight back and escape likely saved my life.

Chapter 14

The True Cost of Rough Sleeping

The trauma that I experienced during that incident, combined with the memories from my time in the orphanage, was incredibly difficult to bear. It is evident that my past experiences compounded my fear and heightened my awareness of the dangers around me.

Around the same time, I remember starting to feel very unwell. The weather was getting colder, and there was no respite from it. With no one to speak to about what the symptoms were, it made me feel helpless, and worried. I had developed an incessant cough that hurt me. People would often look at me in the streets because I would occasionally be spitting up blood. I had a severe pain between my shoulders that would not go away. I was also feeling hot, and cold, often shivering, I felt dizzy as if I were fainting. I put that down to not eating for days.

Was I so ill, that I was heading to the same awful fate that took my lovely Mom?

Not knowing what it was or what to do I made my way to the Birmingham City General Hospital outpatients, where I collapsed on the floor in A & E (Accident & Emergency).

I woke up in such a state, after drifting in and out of consciousness, I was very disoriented and frightened. The haze between consciousness and unconsciousness made it challenging to grasp the severity of the situation or understanding what was happening around me.

The immediate environment—a hospital ward, with medical equipment, unfamiliar faces, and sounds—was overwhelming, so frightening and startling. Recalling those fragmented moments while trying to comprehend the gravity of my situation made it emotionally distressing for me.

The process of piecing together what happened during those unconscious intervals was a slow and confusing journey. However, gradually gaining consciousness signalled the beginning of my recovery phase, albeit a challenging one. I was told by the nursing staff that I was unconscious for four days and it was touch and go if I survived. Given my medical history with Tuberculosis, I was told by the medical team how complicated it was for anyone to recover from pneumonia and pleurisy.

I am sure that my Mom was looking down on me at that time and willing her son to survive.

After spending 10 days in the hospital, where I had gained some much-needed weight, and I began to feel stronger. The hospital arranged for me to continue recuperating at a Salvation Army Hostel until I felt well enough to leave. It was a temporary respite from the harsh realities of life on the streets, a chance to regain my strength and gather my thoughts.

At the hostel, I found peace and a little bit of security in the kindness of strangers and the simple comforts of a warm bed and hot meals. It was a brief reprieve from the uncertainty and hardship that had become all too familiar in my life. For a Moment, I allowed myself to hope for a better future, to believe that things might finally be looking up.

Unfortunately, the stability offered by the hostel was short-lived. It wasn't long before I found myself back on the streets once again, as they felt I was ready to leave, giving some other unfortunate a chance to get help. So, again, I found myself facing the same struggles and uncertainties as before. It was difficult to come to terms with knowing that even the brief respite provided by the hostel couldn't shield me from the harsh realities of life on the streets.

Although the road ahead was uncertain, I refused to lose hope. With determination as my guide, I resolved to keep moving forward, one step at a time, in search of a brighter tomorrow. And while the journey ahead would be filled with challenges and obstacles, I knew that as long as I held onto the memories of home and the love that had sustained me, I would never truly be alone.

In the depths of despair, I clung to my coping mechanisms, music became my go-to, it provided me with an escape from the harsh realities that surrounded me.

I found peace, and encouragement, in the melodies that echoed from (groups, like America who had a hit with "A horse with no name", and the classic "Bridge Over Troubled Waters" by Simon and Garfunkel.

Those records would be playing on the juke box in a café that I would often sit in to keep warm providing a fleeting sense of tranquility amidst the chaos.

Those times were bleak. Any acts of kindness from strangers reminded me that humanity still thrived, even in the darkest corners of society. Those glimmers of optimism provided a flicker of light in the abyss, reminding me that there was more to life than the hardship I currently endured, as there was nothing worse than losing my Mom and Dad.

I endured the trauma of sleeping rough, emerging from the darkness with a newfound appreciation for the simple joys of a warm bed and a sense of security.

My experience on the streets became a testament to the strength of the human spirit and a reminder that even in the face of unimaginable conditions, the seeds of hope can still blossom.

Chapter 15

Avoiding the Gangs and Drugs

Another threat to my safety were the many drug gangs working the cafes and pubs in Birmingham in the 1970s, who often tried to get me to push their drugs in exchange for money, but I did not succumb to their threatening behaviour. I felt that was a major obstacle that I had to deal with on a daily basis. But I realised that if I started working with them then there was only one outlook. Prison!

In the streets of Birmingham during the 1970s, the city was marred by the presence of drug gangs. I found myself at a crossroads. The allure of easy money through involvement in drug pushing was a constant temptation, a shortcut that promised quick riches but threatened to compromise my principles. However, I resisted the siren call of illicit gains, determined to walk a different path.

The city's cafes and pubs became the battlegrounds where drug gangs asserted their influence, attempting to recruit individuals like me into their illicit operations. The pressure to succumb to their coercive tactics was relentless. Offers of money, and to buy me food, and veiled threats, and the coercive atmosphere of the streets became part of my daily reality. Refusing to become entangled in their web, I found myself facing the brunt of physical violence – kicks and punches became the price I paid for standing firm against the tide of criminal temptation.

The bruises from physical altercations were not just wounds on the skin but markers of the resilience required to resist the pull of an easy but perilous path.

The constant confrontation with drug gangs posed a major obstacle that overshadowed my daily life. It was a battle not just against physical aggression but against the pervasive influence of a criminal underworld. The streets, once familiar and communal, now bore the scars of a city struggling against the encroachment of illicit enterprises.

Despite the physical toll exacted by those who sought to draw me into their illicit activities, I held firm to my moral integrity.

I had always been a firm believer that fate played a major part in life, that our destinies were written in the stars long before we ever took our first breath. And yet, as I stumbled blindly through the chaos of the city, I couldn't shake the feeling that perhaps fate was nothing more than a cruel joke, a cosmic puppeteer pulling the strings of our lives with a callous disregard for our hopes and dreams.

Even in the darkest of moments, there was a glimmer of hope, a flicker of light amidst the shadows that threatened to engulf me whole. For as much as fate may have conspired against me, it had also brought me allies in the form of kind strangers and unexpected acts of compassion. So, as I disappeared into the anonymity of the bustling city streets, battered, and bruised but unbroken in spirit, I clung to the belief that fate, for all its capriciousness, had not yet finished writing my story. For though the road ahead may be fraught with peril and uncertainty, I would continue to walk it with courage and determination, trusting that in the end, fate would lead me to where I was meant to be.

As the struggle persisted, my resilience was strong. Triumph over temptation wasn't just a personal victory; it was a victory for moral clarity against the backdrop of a city grappling with the shadows of its own vices. The streets of Birmingham, once synonymous with temptation, became the battleground where my steadfast commitment paved the way for a destiny untethered from the ominous allure of easy money.

My major objective was to look for work, knocking on countless business doors, facing rejection after rejection. But I refused to let setbacks define me. Each "no" only strengthened my resolve to keep pushing forward. Eventually, an opportunity presented itself.

⎯⎯◄❖►⎯⎯

Chapter 16

Fortuitous Encounter

In my local café where there were people that had become familiar faces to me, seeing them every day whilst I was taking respite from the cold, I was approached by one of those familiar faces, a man who asked me if I wanted to do some casual work, cash in hand. I could not believe it; I had secured a casual job working nights cleaning offices in a factory. The chance meeting in the cafe with Albert Davies felt like more than just a coincidence; it was a Moment that seemed to defy the odds and affirm my belief in the guiding hand of fate.

As I sat there, nursing a cup of steaming hot tea and lost in my own thoughts, I noticed a weathered-looking man enter the cafe. His eyes scanned the room before coming to rest on me, and in that instant, I felt a strange sense of recognition, as if we were two pieces of a puzzle destined to fit together.

With a friendly smile, the man approached my table, introducing himself as Albert Davies. His presence was comforting, his demeanour warm and inviting, and before I knew it, we were engaged in a conversation.

As Albert shared his own experiences and struggles with me, I couldn't help but feel a sense of kinship with him. It was as if our lives had been interlinked long before we ever crossed paths in that cafe, connected by threads of fate that stretched across time and space.

Through our conversation, I learned that Albert had faced his own share of challenges and setbacks in life, yet he had emerged stronger and more resilient than ever. His words resonated with me on a profound level, offering a sense of hope and inspiration that I desperately needed in that Moment.

In the days and weeks that followed our chance meeting, Albert became more than just a passing acquaintance; he became a confidant, guiding me through the ups and downs of life with wisdom and compassion. In the short time that I knew him, he came across as a genuine person. Thank God, he found me.

Looking back on that fateful day in the cafe, I am filled with gratitude for the role that Albert Davies has played in my life. He may have entered as a stranger, but he left as a cherished friend, forever etched in my heart as a testament to the power of fate and the unexpected connections that shape our lives. And as I continue on my journey, I do so with the unwavering belief that some meetings are simply meant to be.

I can still remember the first day working. I was shattered by the end of my shift. I soon found my way around and fortunately during breaks I took the opportunity to grab valuable sleep. It was the start of my road to breaking the habit of rough sleeping.

It was a temporary roof over my head, albeit the chance to grab 2 to 3 hours a night of valuable sleep, provided by a man who helped save my life - Albert Davies, of Erdington Industrial Cleaners, to whom I owe a debt of gratitude. I was paid £2.50 per week, which may not sound a great deal of money, but it kept the hunger away, and for 3 to 4 months whilst working there, I was able to gain better health. Without that good fortune God knows what would have happened.

The casual job opportunity that presented itself was like a ray of light breaking through the clouds, offering me a glimmer of hope and the chance to take my first steps towards a brighter future. It provided me with the means to start looking for more permanent employment, and with renewed determination, I set out to pursue opportunities that would allow me to better myself and achieve my long-term goals.

As I began to apply for jobs with higher pay and greater potential for growth, I felt a sense of excitement and anticipation building within me. It wasn't long before my efforts paid off, and I found myself landing a position that offered not only better pay but also the opportunity to learn and grow in a more challenging environment.

Each new opportunity that came my way, I seized it with both hands, eager to prove myself and demonstrate my worth. But even as I worked diligently to excel in my current role, I never lost sight of my ultimate aspirations. I knew that the initial jobs I took were only stepping stones on my journey towards more demanding white-collar roles, and I was determined to keep pushing myself forward, no matter how challenging the path ahead might be.

I pursued further education and training, eager to enhance my qualifications and position myself for success in the competitive world of white-collar employment.

Beyond the pursuit of professional advancement, there was also a deeper desire within me to better myself in every aspect of my life. I sought to cultivate a growth mindset, constantly pushing myself to learn and evolve, both personally and professionally. I embraced challenges as opportunities for growth and saw setbacks as valuable learning experiences that would ultimately make me stronger and more resilient.

So, with each passing day, I moved closer to realising my dreams, fuelled by a relentless drive to succeed and a steadfast belief in my own potential. The initial jobs that I took may have been short-term in nature, but they laid the foundation for a future filled with endless possibilities and the promise of greater success yet to come.

Balancing work and reading were a challenging juggling act, but I refused to let fatigue or doubt deter me. I knew that education was my ticket to a brighter future. I would read all the financial newspapers that were in the reception area of the factory when I could get hold of them, from back to front, and as many books from the library on Finance and Economics that I could.

I knew deep within me that education held the key to unlocking a brighter future, a future filled with opportunities and possibilities beyond the confines of my current circumstances.

With each article I read, each market report I analysed, I gained valuable insights into the world of finance and economics, slowly piecing together a mosaic of knowledge that would serve as the foundation for my future success.

Beyond the acquisition of knowledge, my journey was also one of empowerment. With each new insight I gained, each concept I mastered, I felt a renewed sense of confidence and self-assurance. I knew that education was not just about acquiring information; it was about empowering myself to shape my own destiny, to carve out a path towards a future filled with promise and possibility.

So, armed with the knowledge and skills I had acquired, I set out to pursue my dreams with unwavering determination. I knew that the road ahead would be challenging, filled with obstacles and setbacks, but I also knew that with education as my ally, there was no limit to what I could achieve. For me, education was not just a ticket to a brighter future; it was the key that unlocked the door to endless possibilities and the promise of a life filled with purpose and fulfilment.

After several months, at the age of twenty, I had saved enough money to rent a room. It was the best thing that had happened to me. I started to further my horizons, and by chance met up with my twin brother again, whom I had not seen for over four years. I heard that he was engaged to be married and had his own two-bedroom council flat on the other side of the city. He asked me to move in with him.

Chapter 17

Looking back at the start of Another Journey.

In those early days, I had so many jobs, and for whatever reason, I could not last more than a few weeks.

It was not that I was lazy, or anything, I just felt that I was better than doing factory work. No disrespect to factory work.

I had made a lot of new friends, and one in particular, Paddy, who had itchy feet, and was always talking about leaving, and travelling. The chance came for him when he received a substantial legacy from his grandmother. It enabled him to pass his driving test and buy a second-hand car. That was his licence to go and explore the world. In our many conversations he had told me that he hated living in Birmingham, and he asked if I would go with him. I said, "Why not?"

For some reason, Paddy had always been fascinated with the idea of exploring Jersey in the Channel Islands. Perhaps it was the allure of a different culture, or the promise of a unique adventure. Intrigued by his enthusiasm, we decided to make Jersey our base for the summer.

Upon arriving, we quickly secured jobs at a local pub. I found myself in the kitchen, adapting to the cooking facilities and the diverse pub menu. The skills I had picked up during my time in the orphanage kitchen turned out to be more valuable than I had anticipated, making the transition smoother than expected.

Our summer at the pub turned out to be nothing short of fantastic. The vibrant atmosphere, coupled with the friendship between Paddy and me, made it a memorable season. Part of our compensation included the use of an old caravan for accommodation. Little did we know that this would spark an idea that would shape the next chapter of our lives.

As autumn set in, Paddy and I found ourselves drawn to a unique project. The old caravan provided by the pub owner became the canvas for our dreams. Paddy, with his background as an apprentice engineer, brought a wealth of skills to the table. We spent months meticulously reconfiguring the caravan into the perfect Burger Van, painting it a distinctive combination of red and white.

Inside, we carefully planned every detail. A fridge, grill, oven and a boiler were installed. We even reinforced the floor area to meet fire regulations and added toilet facilities. The transformation was nothing short of miraculous. Our dream was now a tangible reality, and all that remained was to embark on our journey back to the UK.

Agreeing on roles, I took on the position of chef, responsible for the culinary aspect of our venture, while Paddy assumed the role of driver and assistant server. The prospect of adventure was exhilarating, and as we boarded the ferry to England, the world was our oyster. With no fixed plan, our strategy was simple – target major events where crowds gathered.

However, the excitement was soon met with a challenge we had not anticipated. The weight of the caravan became a significant hurdle. Our 2-litre

Ambassador struggled to pull the 22-foot vehicle, prompting us to make a quick decision on changing our mode of transportation.

In 1982 with combined savings of £1500 earmarked for fuel, food, and living expenses, we faced a tough decision. Paddy's second-hand car, valued at £375, was not up to the task. The acquisition of a second-hand Land Rover at £750 meant dipping into our savings and adjusting our plans. Devastating as it was, it forced us to start our events a month earlier than we had initially intended.

The road ahead held uncertainty, but it also brimmed with the promise of excitement, adventure, unknown challenges, and the fulfilment of a dream we had meticulously planned during those months of transforming the caravan. Little did we know that this journey would redefine the course of our lives.

We were relieved that the transport was sorted, and we had started to plan the first of several stops up and down the UK. One of the memories still stuck in my mind was our visit to the Derby Racehorse Meeting at Epsom in England.

Our journey took an exciting turn as we arrived at the Epsom Derby, a four-day spectacle of horse racing. The anticipation in the air was palpable as we pitched our vibrant Red and White Burger Van on the picturesque Epsom Downs. Surrounded by the natural beauty of the downs, our little corner became a hub of activity, enticing both seasoned racegoers and curious onlookers.

The atmosphere at the Epsom Derby was electric. The rolling hills of Epsom Downs provided a breathtaking backdrop to the thrilling races. As the horses thundered down the track, the cheers and excitement of the crowd filled the air.

Our Burger Van, of which we were both so proud, adorned in its distinctive colours, became a beacon amidst the sea of all racegoers.

As the aroma of fried onions, sizzling burgers and hot dogs wafted through the air, we found ourselves at the heart of a culinary adventure. The response from customers was overwhelming, and our carefully planned menu featuring teas, coffees, sandwiches, and, of course, our signature burgers, was met with enthusiasm. The spirit at the event was infectious, and we became a focal point for those seeking both a culinary delight and a sense of community. Even overnight, we fed the local police and security. Amidst the hustle and bustle of the Epsom Derby, we forged unexpected connections. Racing enthusiasts and food lovers alike gathered around our Burger Van, sharing stories, laughter, and the joy of a shared experience. The atmosphere extended beyond the racetrack, creating bonds that transcended the typical vendor-customer relationship.

However, our time at Epsom Derby was not without its challenges. Managing the demand for our culinary offerings and navigating the logistics of a major event presented hurdles. Yet, with each challenge, we found a solution. I remember us running out of Bacon and Sausage on our second day, and I had to walk 3 miles to the local butchers to buy more. The sense of triumph at the end of each day, having served a multitude of satisfied customers, fuelled our determination to tackle the road ahead.

As the Epsom Derby concluded, we took a Moment to reflect on the journey so far. The success at this major event fuelled our aspirations for the future. The decision to start our events earlier than planned became a blessing in disguise, allowing us to assess our mettle at one of the grandest racing events in the UK.

With the Epsom Derby behind us, our journey continued. The road stretched out before us, winding through towns and cities, each presenting its unique set of challenges and opportunities. Our Burger Van, once a dream on the Jersey shores, now carried with it the stories of Epsom Downs, a Wembley Cup Final, an Ayr Gold Cup, the bonds formed, and the taste of success that fuelled our aspirations for the adventures yet to come.

Our journey took an unexpected turn when we found ourselves in Great Yarmouth on the east coast of England. The picturesque coastal town became the backdrop for a challenge we had not anticipated—mechanical problems with our trusty Land Rover. The elusive part we needed for repairs could only be found in a small village near Great Yarmouth.

As we navigated the repairs, little did I know that this Moment would mark a significant divergence in our paths. Paddy, who had met someone special during our Scottish adventures, expressed a desire to move there and be with her. The decision to part ways was bittersweet, as it created a sense of loss. The friendship that had fuelled our journey was now making way for individual pursuits. So, off he went in pursuit of love and life with this young lady. I cannot lie, I felt at a loss when he left.

Chapter 18

Alone in Great Yarmouth England

I wandered the seafront, contemplating the road ahead. It was during this, that I stumbled upon a game-changing opportunity.

An advertisement in a newsagent's window caught my eye—it sought someone to run a Fish and Chips shop, providing food to a club within a Holiday Camp in the nearby seaside resort of Hemsby Great Yarmouth.

I called the number on the card in the window and had a conversation with the owner of the site. His name was Rodney. Two days later, I found myself sitting across from him and his advisors discussing the prospect of running the concession.

To my surprise the offer was granted to me. It marked the end of my on-the-road adventures with our beloved Burger Van, as a new chapter awaited in the world of fish & chips.

As I accepted the concession in Hemsby, I could not help but reflect on the winding journey that had brought me to this point.

The Burger Van, once a symbol of adventure and friendship, would now find its final resting place. I decided to advertise it, and I had lots of interested customers. I sold it and the sale proceeds provided me with enough money after Paddy's share to support the opening of the new Fish and Chip shop.

The open road that stretched before me during those days of exploration now transformed into the stability of a seaside business.

The transition from a nomadic lifestyle to a settled existence in Hemsby brought its own set of challenges. Navigating the nuances of a fish & chip shop and providing food to the vibrant club within the Holiday Camp marked a new chapter in my culinary journey. I had to learn to fry fish! What a challenge that was! I asked a local Greek fish and chip shop owner called Sharble, if he would show me how to fillet fish and teach me to fry fish and chips. I was so surprised how many burns I got in the first few attempts, but I quickly got the hang of it. Soon I was an expert ready to take on the challenge of 600 chalets on the holiday site.

The sights and sounds of the seaside resort became the backdrop to a life that, although different from the adventures on the road, carried its own promise of growth and fulfilment.

As I took on the unexpected turn my journey had taken, I understood that life had a way of unfolding in ways we least expect. The sense of loss from parting with Paddy and the Burger Van gradually gave way to the anticipation of new opportunities and the promise of a different adventure—a chapter that unfolded along the scenic shores of Hemsby. I had taken on the lease in early winter some 5 months before the start of the holiday season. The concession to my horror was badly in need of tender loving care, it was no surprise how dirty it was, as it had been closed for over two years.

As I embarked on my new venture running a fish & chip shop and a catering franchise to a night club within a Holiday Camp, I found unexpected support in the form of my younger brother, Vince, a highly intelligent and quick-witted individual, who became my trusted assistant for the first season.

Vince's brilliance was evident in his ability to complete "The Times Crossword" in a mere 10 minutes—an intellectual feat that left me in awe of him. However, alongside his intelligence, I recognised a sense of vulnerability that I had witnessed previously.

Before his journey to Hemsby, Vince had fallen into a crowd back in Birmingham that was into drugs, and where heavy drinking was prevalent. My duty, as I promised to my Mom, was to look after him, to guide him away from the dangers that lurked in his path.

Upon learning about Vince's involvement with a group that indulged in drugs and excessive drinking, my heart sank. It became clear that my time in Hemsby would not only be about running a fish & chip shop but also about steering my younger brother away from a potentially destructive path. Vince's lack of ambition to take on the world had led him down a perilous road, and my challenge was to bring him back, to show him the potential for growth beyond the shadows of his past.

The winter months became a period of building a new relationship for both of us.

Together, we meticulously cleaned and organised the place to meet the Local Council's stringent standards for a 5-star cleanliness rating.

The licence to operate hinged on this accomplishment. It was during these cold months that the bond between us strengthened, and the determination to create a successful business became our shared goal.

As we approached the opening of our fish & chip shop, at the end of May 1983 Vince's dedication and support proved invaluable. He was not just a brother; he was a dependable partner in this venture. Vince's watchful eye ensured the smooth running of the business, and his desire to contribute to its success surpassed all expectations. Together, we faced the challenges that came with a bustling seaside resort, and Vince's commitment became the driving force behind our daily operations.

Operating a business in a seaside resort demanded resilience and adaptability. Vince's role extended beyond being my brother; he became an integral part of the team, watching my back and ensuring the place ran seamlessly.

The unspoken understanding between us went beyond the responsibilities of work. It was a shared commitment to a better future for Vince, away from the shadows of his past. As the business flourished under our joint efforts, so did our relationship.

The promise I made to my Mom—to look after him—had evolved into a journey of growth, redemption, and the revival of ambition in the heart of a brother who, for a while, had lost his way.

Our shared triumph became the foundation for a chapter in our lives that revitalised not only the fish & chip shop but also the essence of familial support and resilience.

That first summer was a fantastic success. I was so proud of myself and Vince.

The echoes of our first summer in Hemsby reverberated with success. It was a season beyond our wildest dreams, where we not only met but exceeded every expectation, consistently surpassing our targets month after month. The sense of achievement was not only mine but belonged to the entire team that had poured their hearts into making our fish & chip shop, and night club a thriving success.

As a gesture of gratitude for the hard work and dedication displayed by our team, everyone received a well-deserved bonus. The friendship that had developed over the summer months transformed into a shared celebration. Closing the doors of the fish & chip shop at the end of October that year was not just a seasonal transition; it was a Moment to reflect on the collective success that had been achieved.

With the onset of autumn, our focus shifted to the Variety Club—a winter weekend venue that brought a new dimension to our endeavours. The club, owned by the site proprietor, became a magnet for top celebrities, attracting the crème de la crème of comedians and singers to entertain a lively audience of 500 every Friday and Saturday night.

I vividly recall the star-studded evenings where top comedians and singers of their time graced the stage, turning the Variety Club into a spectacle of entertainment.

Our team seamlessly moved from fish & chips to serving a diverse menu, including basket-style meals and delectable steak and chips options. The energy within the club matched the excitement of the summer, creating an atmosphere that was both electric and unforgettable.

The Variety Club was a popular entertainment venue; it became a versatile space used for weddings as well. Our team took on the responsibility of providing catering services, crafting buffets that added a touch of culinary excellence to these special occasions.

As winter unfolded, we found ourselves navigating the challenges and delights of the Club. The winter months, filled with laughter, music and celebrations, sustained us until the arrival of May— the signal for a new beginning.

With the first blooms of spring, we prepared to welcome a new summer, marking the cyclic nature of our culinary adventures in Hemsby.

The shut doors of the fish & chip shop during winter served not as an end but as a hiatus—a period of rest and strategic planning. The success of the Club and its varied offerings lifted our spirits, laying the groundwork for another summer of adventures. The cycle of closure and renewal became the rhythm of our journey, each season building upon the successes of the last, creating a legacy and along the scenic shores of Hemsby. The way of life for me in Great Yarmouth was very frugal and I was never exuberant with money, always thinking back to the time on the streets when money was your survival ticket. One of my jobs every week was to take all the laundry from the kitchen to the local launderette in the village on a Sunday Morning, as it was often the quietest day of the week.

It was there one Sunday on 12th August 1984 that I met a girl who I would end up marrying. For years, I found myself avoiding the intimacy and vulnerability that romantic relationships often entailed.

The pain and trauma I experienced as a child created a barrier between me and the prospect of forming intimate relationships, as I grappled with feelings of shame, guilt, and fear. Struggling with my own identity and sexual orientation, I found it challenging to reconcile the past experiences with my desires for love, companionship and understanding. The scars left by the abuse made it difficult for me to trust and open up to others, fearing the potential for further pain and exploitation.

While understanding my own sexuality was a challenging and complex one, my journey of self-acceptance and healing led me to a place of greater self-awareness and self-compassion. Life has its share of surprises, and sometimes, in the most unexpected places, destiny unveils its grand plans. I invite you to step into the world where I crossed paths with the love of my life, Angie – a serendipitous encounter that would forever shape the course of my heart.

I now know and believe that Love often has a way of finding us when we least expect it. Such was the case when our paths first converged. It was as if the universe conspired to orchestrate a chance meeting, weaving its threads through the fabric of time to bring us together. Our first encounter was unremarkable, just two souls brushing against each other in the vast tapestry of life.

Yet, even in that ordinary Moment, there was a spark. A spark that ignited curiosity, a connection that felt oddly familiar. It was like recognising a melody from a distant memory, a melody that had been waiting to be played again.

❦

Chapter 19

Meeting the Love of my Life and Soulmate, Angie

My encounter with Angie in the launderette on the 12th of August 1984 was a moment that would change my life forever. As I stood there, going about my daily routine, I was captivated by the sight of Angie walking through the door. Her beauty and presence struck me instantly, and a profound feeling washed over me. The lasting impact of Angie's beauty and her hourglass figure will remain etched in my memories until the day I die. I will always remember the time and place where we met as it has left an indelible mark on my journey. I am grateful to the powers above to have allowed me to encounter someone so uniquely beautiful.

Angie's impact on my life was instant. She was confident and forward thinking; in a way she reminded me so much of my Mom.

Intrigued by her kind gesture of offering newspapers to everyone, I could not resist the opportunity to engage in conversation. With a touch of humour and charm, I playfully asked if she was buying and expressed my interest in accepting the offer. Angie, perhaps a bit taken aback by my response, responded affirmatively, signalling the start of a connection that would grow deeper with time.

From that brief interaction, I sensed a special connection between us. I could not shake the feeling that Angie was meant to be a part of my life, and a seed of certainty was planted in my heart. There was something about her that resonated deeply within me, and I knew in my soul that our paths were meant to be.

The newspaper cupid strikes! Who would have thought that a bundle of printed words could lead to a romance story that rivals all those cheesy rom coms?

So, there I was, the hero, Mr. Smooth Operator. Noticing Angie's generous newspaper distribution, I decided to turn on the charm like a light switch.

With a twinkle in my eye and a dash of wit that could make Shakespeare jealous, I managed to pop the question – the "Are you buying newspapers?" I mean, who needs pick-up lines when you have the world of print media at your disposal? Then, on cue, the unexpected twist in the tale.

Angie, a bit like a deer caught in headlights, managed to utter a surprised "yes". Maybe it was the shock of being offered a newspaper exchange instead of a date, which caught her off guard, hey, who can blame her? Newspaper-based flirtation was not exactly in the dating manual.

So, the seeds of connection were planted, watered with a sprinkle of humour and newspaper ink. What started as a quirky exchange blossomed into something deeper – a connection that could not be explained by mere words or headlines. It was like destiny had tossed the two characters into the same storyline, and there was no escaping the twist of fate.

Angie had two young children. Lisa aged 3 and a half, and Philip aged just 2 years.

From that Moment, a magical sensation danced in the air, something that said, "Hey, you two, get ready for an adventure that will rival the crossword puzzles in the Times." It was like the universe decided to give us a nudge and whisper, "Get ready, lovebirds, your paths were meant to cross."

As we continued to spend time together, the bond grew stronger. We shared laughter, deep conversations, and countless moments that solidified our connection. Our love story blossomed, and we became inseparable.

Through the "Ups and Downs" and difficulties of life, we have stood by each other's side, supporting, and loving one another unconditionally. We have navigated challenges together, celebrated victories together, and built a life filled with love, trust and shared dreams.

Angie became not only my partner but also my best friend and confidante. We shared a profound understanding and a deep connection that transcended the superficial. We laughed together, cried together, and created a haven of love and warmth within our relationship.

Our journey was not without its challenges, but our commitment to each other remained unwavering. Through thick and thin, we have faced life's obstacles together, finding solace and strength in our unwavering love and companionship.

I knew in my heart that Angie was the woman that I had been waiting for, the love of my life. The chance encounter in the launderette had turned into a lifelong partnership, filled with joy, love, and a profound sense of fulfilment. Our love story was a testament to the power of fate and the magic that can unfold when two souls find each other in the most unexpected places.

Who needs candlelit dinners and romantic walks on the beach when you can meet the love of your life in a place that smells like detergent and adventure? It is like destiny thought, "You know what would be a great idea? A meet-cute with a side of fabric softener!"

Let us not forget the magic – that sweet, detergent-scented magic! It is like the universe decided to add a sprinkle of fairy dust to the laundry detergent, turning ordinary clothes-washing into a Cinderella story for the ages. Who knew that the secret to finding love was hiding in our laundry basket all along?

So, as you fold your socks and remember that fateful day in the launderette, just know that your love story is like a romantic comedy that even Hollywood would envy. It has unexpected places, charming mishaps, and enough laughter to rival a stand-up comedy show. Who needs fancy romantic settings when you have the spin cycle of destiny on your side?

My love for Angie extended beyond our romantic connection. When I entered Angie's life, I not only embraced her but also embraced her two beautiful children, Lisa and Philip, as if they were my own. In my heart, I knew that love knew no boundaries and that family was not defined solely by blood.

We talked about our past and she was very candid about her previous relationship, and the experiences in her first marriage that were deeply traumatic, and no doubt has left lasting scars on her. The physical and sexual abuse she endured at the hands of her ex-husband had not only inflicted visible wounds but also inflicted deep emotional and psychological pain, as she endured the threats not only to her safety, but also that of her two young children. Despite the challenges she faced, Angie's resilience shone through as she bravely confronted her past.

As our relationship developed and grew stronger, with open arms and a loving heart, I took on the role of a father figure to Lisa and Philip. I welcomed them into my life, providing them with a sense of stability, support and unconditional love. Together, we formed a blended family, built on the foundation of trust, respect and genuine affection.

My decision to adopt Lisa and Philip was an expression of my deep love for Angie and my commitment to the family's unity. It was a choice that went beyond legalities, as it symbolised my desire to be a devoted father to them and to create a nurturing and loving environment where we could thrive.

As the years passed, the bond between us, Lisa and Philip grew stronger. We shared countless memories, experiences, and milestones as a family.

My love for them was unwavering, and I embraced the joys and challenges of parenthood with dedication and enthusiasm.

Through my actions, I exemplified the true meaning of family, showing that love knows no bounds and that the connection between a parent and a child goes far beyond biology. Lisa and Philip, in turn, found solace, support and a deep sense of belonging in the love and care that I showered upon them.

My decision to adopt Lisa and Philip not only transformed our lives but also enriched my own. Our relationship was a testament to the power of love and united by the bonds of love that we shared through our journey.

Losing our baby, Thomas, even before birth, was a heart-wrenching experience. Our memory was marked by both joys and sorrows.

We had made so many plans and preparations for the arrival of our baby boy. The loss of Thomas meant the loss of dreams and aspirations for our family's future.

Coping with the loss of a child often involves a complex process of grieving, because we lived so far away from family and friends. We had no support to navigate this difficult period and find ways to heal. It was an awful time for us both.

While the loss of Thomas has undoubtedly left a lasting scar, it is possible that it also strengthened the bond between us as a couple. Going through such a loss together can reinforce love for each other during challenging times.

It is also important to acknowledge that the loss of a child, at any stage of pregnancy, is a deeply personal and unique experience. The grief and healing process can vary greatly from one person to another. While the pain of our loss will never completely disappear, over time, it often becomes more manageable.

The memory of Thomas will always remain a part of our family story, a reminder of the strength of mind that carried us through that challenging time.

Chapter 20

Fifth Person in Our Family

I remember coming home from work and being greeted by the news of Angie's pregnancy. Our hearts were filled with joy and anticipation. I remember being nervous for weeks on end in the initial stages. As the months passed, we eagerly awaited the arrival of our baby, cherishing every Moment and embracing the wonder of a new life. Finally, the day came when our prayers were answered, and Julie, a beautiful baby girl, entered our lives.

Julie brought a newfound sense of completeness to the family. We embraced our roles as loving parents, dedicating ourselves to providing a nurturing and supportive environment for Julie to thrive.

As we watched her grow, I found renewed motivation to be successful in life.

My children became my driving force, inspiring me to work tirelessly to create a better future for the family. I saw in my children the embodiment of our love and the embodiment of hope, a constant reminder of the importance of resilience and determination.

Angie was a wonderful Mom, and although she was a disciplinarian our children loved her. We both agreed that having certain rules around which our family functioned would benefit everyone. We could take our children anywhere and people would comment on how well behaved they were. They loved the praise.

My aspirations and dreams became intertwined with the well-being and happiness of my family. Julie's presence further instilled in me a sense of purpose, fuelling my ambition. It bought back memories of my own childhood of being a provider for my siblings.

With Julie in our lives, I experienced a deepened sense of gratitude and appreciation. I treasured every milestone, every laugh, and every shared Moment, cherishing the precious gift of family that we had been blessed with.

Her presence not only completed our family but also served as a reminder of the enduring power of love. We faced life's trials and triumphs as a united front, drawing strength from our unwavering bond and cherishing the incredible gift of family that God had granted us. Around that time, Angie and I talked about her desire to return to the Midlands to be closer to her parents. The decision weighed heavily on me, considering I had a stable income from the concession, and now three mouths to feed. I struggled with the idea at first but felt that if Angie was not contented living in Great Yarmouth then I should support her feelings.

I also considered that the concession had no tangible value, as the business was not mine to sell. After some soul searching I reached out to the concession owner and shared my intentions. We came to an agreement, and I committed to staying on for a month to assist in him finding a suitable replacement. The uncertainty of this period cast a shadow over our family, given that my expertise in catering, though self-taught, lacked formal qualifications. Whilst I was proficient to a certain level, the absence of a qualifying certificate hindered my ability to secure a salary sufficient for long-term support.

With my primary source of income now severed, I found myself effectively unemployed. Faced with this challenge, I decided to explore alternative career paths. I ventured into the realm of job interviews, primarily targeting opportunities in sales. Lacking experience in most industries, I eventually found myself applying for positions in the insurance sector. The shift into a new field brought its own set of challenges, as I was stepping into unfamiliar territory. However, it became a necessary step in my quest to secure a stable and sustainable source of income for our family. The journey into the insurance sector marked a significant departure from my culinary background, but it reflected my determination to adapt and provide for my family in the face of unexpected changes.

The first few months of moving back to the Midlands was fraught with challenges. Having to live with Angie's parents was not ideal, the house was overcrowded and that in itself led to friction. They were great people and helped us to find our own house.

⸻◆⸻

Chapter 21

Navigating the Business Landscape: From Dreams to Realities

In the world of commerce, dreams can be transformed into tangible realities, and aspirations can take flight as successful enterprises.

The business landscape was no gentle terrain; it was a wilderness of ups and downs. There were moments when setbacks threatened to derail my progress, but each setback was a lesson. I was learning to pivot, to recalibrate strategies, and to forge ahead with a renewed sense of determination.

My determination to create a better life for myself, and my children, served as a constant guiding light, pushing me forward.

I started work in Life Insurance sales. I remember it was December, the winter that year was colder than usual. I had only one suit, and that was second hand, and I owned one tie. I relied for transport solely on my father-in-law, George, who drove me to appointments.

From the first Moment I stepped into the family fold, George, my father-in-law, welcomed me with open arms. His warmth and genuine interest in getting to know me created a foundation of trust. It was not just about being a part of the family; it was about becoming a trusted companion on life's journey.

One of the most significant lessons I learned from George was the importance of patience and understanding. He had a way of diffusing tensions with a well-timed joke or a story from his own experiences. His ability to unravel the complexities of family life with grace and humour became a guiding light for me, especially during those early days.

As a father-in-law, George played a pivotal role in shaping my perspective personally on marriage. Through his actions, he demonstrated the value of mutual respect and support. His commitment to family became a blueprint for the kind of partner and parent I aspired to be. He loved his daughter and his grandchildren, and he would be on hand at any time.

But it was not just about the serious stuff. George had a playful side that added a lightness to family gatherings. Whether it was sharing amusing anecdotes from his past or engaging in friendly banter, he knew how to create an atmosphere of joy and togetherness.

His legacy as a father-in-law is not just in the lessons he imparted but, in the love, laughter, and enduring connections that continue to shape the family he helped build.

After applying for many jobs and being rejected because of lack of experience, I managed to secure a job with Canada Life, an Insurance Company, specialising in Life Policies, and Investments. It was a commission only offer. I remember that the sales manager said that I had to wear a suit and tie before I could start work.

The job meant that I had to do a huge amount of cold calling, knocking on doors asking people if they wanted to buy any life insurance. I was working on commission only back then, often working 12-hour days. I recall that people were more receptive to the method of cold calling in the late seventies. However, I did suffer abuse and some of the language aimed at me on the doorstep was unbelievable. With George's help, I bought an old Volvo, which was not very dependable, and more often than not on freezing days on my way to meetings it would break down. I would sit in the car with my head in my hands and cry with frustration because, it would mean that I had to cancel meetings on those days, so no money was earned.

It was exceedingly difficult to raise a family on commission only. Some weeks I would earn nothing and others barely enough to pay the rent.

Facing poor results and the looming threat of losing my job was a daunting and stressful situation. It was a moment that demanded creativity, resilience, and a willingness to think outside the box in order to turn the tide in my favour.

I found out at a monthly meeting, that I was at the bottom of the office, the pressure to find a solution mounted with each passing day. I was embarrassed, and dreaded telling Angie, that I was faced with the prospect of being sacked.

I refused to be defeated, instead I chose to channel my energy into finding a new approach that would yield better results and would gain me access to people who needed to buy our products.

I began to explore alternative strategies, scouring my mind for how to sell a product that would set me apart from the competition. And then, like a bolt of lightning the inspiration struck.

I thought that rather than relying on cold calls to generate leads, I would leverage my skills to offer a valuable service to a niche market.

By reaching out to school governors and parents, I proposed an opportunity for them to save money for their children's school fees, tapping into a pressing need and offering a solution that resonated deeply with my target audience. We offered a 10 year savings plan which allowed customers to save monthly. To my amazement, my school fees strategy paid off in ways that I could never have imagined. Month after month, I found myself writing an impressive number of policies—20, 30, or more—far surpassing my previous performance and catapulting me to the top of the monthly performance tables.

Yet, perhaps the most surprising aspect of my early success was the fact that I had kept my winning formula a closely guarded secret from my colleagues, who were left dumbfounded by my meteoric rise. Despite their scepticism, I had defied the odds and achieved what seemed impossible, all through my ingenuity, perseverance, and willingness to think outside the box. I knew back then that I had the formula to succeed.

My story serves as a powerful reminder that success often lies not in following the conventional path, but in daring to chart your own course and embracing the possibilities that come with thinking differently. And as I continued to build upon my achievements, my journey stands as a testament to the transformative power of innovation and resilience, when all else seems lost.

As well as working, I would spend every spare hour at night, studying for the Chartered Institute of Insurance Exams, as I realised that qualifications were the key to better job opportunities in the insurance sector. It took me 18 months of serious study before I felt confident enough to sit the exams. I was surprised that I passed all 3 papers first time round which was a very difficult achievement. It did mean that I could now apply for jobs with a salary. The basic salary was a lifeline as it would cover all incidental household expenses.

It was not long before I started to excel, and within the first year of joining my new company, I was offered a promotion to consultant. That meant I would be given a portfolio of existing clients to look after. No more cold calling. Shortly afterwards I was promoted again to trainee manager and then soon after to Local Manager. Along with the responsibility came more salary, and for the first time I was given a company car allowance and other benefits. Life started to feel good, but I took nothing for granted.

I thought to myself, who is now climbing the ladder of business success like a champion! From the bottom rung to the top. I had gone from the office new boy to the office to office manager.

Along with the promotions came the rewards – of annual conferences and travel to foreign lands. And let us be real, you are talking to someone who used to think international cuisine meant trying out a new pizza restaurant. Now I am jet-setting like a pro, navigating airports and pretending I know what "duty-free" really means.

I had gone from basics to the good stuff. My wallet knew the joy of splurging on things that do not have the word "discount" slapped on them.

Let us not forget the star of the show – the insurance industry. It was like my business fairy godmother, waving its policy wand and making sure, that me and my family were well taken care of. Suddenly, I am not just climbing ladders; I am on the way to building a castle, one policy at a time.

⋯⊸⊱⟨ ⟩⊰⊷⋯

Chapter 22

Growth and Fulfilment

My success was not just measured in promotions and business glory. I started to build personal wealth now, and I am like a money magician, turning pence into pounds with the flick of a wrist. It was like I found the secret stash of the finance world.

Along with the challenging work of business, came the rewards of us being able to buy our first home together. It was a monumental achievement, a tangible symbol of the dedication and hard work.

The Moment we held the keys to our own home was a pivotal Momone. It meant that we had an element of security in our lives. The decision to invest in a home marked not just a financial milestone but a deeply personal one.

The process of finding and purchasing that first home was a blend of excitement and anticipation. From scouring estate agents' offices to walking through potential houses, each step brought us closer to a place that we could call our own.

The house we chose together became a canvas for our dreams and a sanctuary. It was more than just four walls and a roof; it reflected our journey, a tangible representation of the love, hard work, and shared accomplishments that defined our relationship.

Owning our first home together was not just about acquiring property; it was about building a foundation for the life we were creating.

In the grand narrative of my autobiography, this chapter stands out as a symbol of success and stability. The home that we built together, the dreams we dared to chase and the rewards that came from our unwavering commitment to each other and our shared aspirations.

How did I get here? Endeavours, determination, and probably a dash of caffeine-induced inspiration. I was like a business superhero, fighting my way to the top with spreadsheets instead of capes.

As my children were growing up and were at an age where I felt that I could do this for myself, the decision to venture into business on my own account was significant and a life-changing step. I had reached the point where I felt comfortable, and after discussing the whole idea with Angie, we were both confident that starting our own business was a pivotal Moment in our lives. After years of successfully building wealth for corporate employers, I realised that it was time to direct my efforts towards creating financial security and independence for myself and my family.

With a desire for greater control over my financial future and the opportunity to reap the rewards of my hard work directly, I felt confidence in my ability, and a willingness to take on the challenges and responsibilities that come with entrepreneurship.

Starting a business requires careful planning, market research, and the ability to identify viable opportunities. It also demands dedication, perseverance, and the willingness to adapt to changing circumstances. My experience in the insurance corporate world provided me with valuable insights, business acumen, and a strong work ethic that would prove beneficial in my new entrepreneurial endeavour.

The journey of entrepreneurship is unique for every individual and business, and it often entails both triumphs and challenges. However, by making the decision to pursue my dreams, I was looking forward to the opportunity to control my own destiny and build a future on my own terms.

Leaving behind stable and secure high-profile positions, and a large salary in a corporate environment can be daunting, as it often involves embracing uncertainty and taking calculated risks. However, I had experience, and a first-class track record of success that played a crucial role in my decision-making process.

My employers recognised my value and fought extremely hard to keep me, which further attests my capabilities and potential for success. So, the time came for Angie, and I to start our own empire. We were fortunate to have had clients who were willing to join us in our venture.

Chapter 23

Looking Forward with Hope and Optimism

Starting the journey of building our own empire with Angie was an exhilarating chapter in our lives. The transition from being an individual contributor to a business owner brings a mix of excitement and challenges, and the fact that we had the support of clients wanting to share our venture was quite the testament to the trust that I had built up in my professional relationships.

As Angie and I ventured into this new phase of our lives, the support of our initial clients became the cornerstone of our business. Their willingness to not only believe in our vision but also invest their trust, and resources, spoke volumes about the reputation we had built.

The early days of our venture were a blend of ridiculously hard work, strategic planning, and a touch of ambitious spirit. With Angie by my side, we managed the intricacies of entrepreneurship, learning and adapting as we went. The synergy between our vision and the needs of our clients fuelled the growth of our business.

This chapter of my life marks a pivotal Moment— the transition from being a part of something to creating something of my own. The clients who joined me in this endeavour became not just business partners but long-life friends, contributing to the foundation of the business that Angie and I were building. The journey ahead was uncertain, but with the support of these early allies, it held the promise of growth, success, and the fulfilment of shared dreams.

Over the years, that followed, we were very successful. We had started to build a business that through renewal income from client's investments, covered all of our business, and living expenses and more.

Along with success came reward.

I was able to pursue my love of horses, and particularly horse racing.

Owning racehorses was more than just a hobby; it was a passion for me that brought immense joy and fulfilment into my life. The world of horseracing captivated me, from the exhilaration of watching my own horses compete to the friendships shared with fellow owners and enthusiasts. It was within this vibrant community that I found a sense of belonging and formed lasting connections.

They say that you meet people for a reason, and that is certainly true in my case, because although I had a little knowledge of the sport, and my expertise was somewhat lacking, a pivotal Moment in my journey towards horse racing came about through a serendipitous encounter with a man who would become an integral part of my life for over three decades. His name was Roy Reeves, a streetwise entrepreneur with a keen eye for the intricacies of the racing world. Our paths crossed unexpectedly, whilst on holiday in the Canary Islands. The impact of our meeting would shape my future in ways I could never have anticipated.

Roy possessed a wealth of knowledge about the inner workings of the racing industry, and he generously shared his insights with me, igniting a passion within me that would soon become all-consuming. From the Moment we met, I was captivated by his stories of triumphs and tribulations on the racetrack, and I found myself drawn deeper into the allure of the sport.

Under Roy's guidance, I embarked on a journey of discovery, immersing myself in the art and science of horse racing. He taught me the finer points of handicapping, the strategies behind successful wagering, and the nuances of horse breeding and training. With each passing day, my appreciation for the sport grew, fuelled by Roy's unwavering enthusiasm and boundless expertise.

But our relationship extended far beyond the realm of horse racing. Roy became not only my mentor but also a trusted confidant and loyal friend. Together, we weathered the highs and lows of life, celebrating victories and offering solace in defeat. His wisdom and guidance were a constant source of strength and inspiration, shaping not only my approach to racing but also my outlook on life itself.

As the years unfolded, Roy remained a steadfast presence by my side, guiding me through the ever-changing landscape of the racing world. Through his mentorship, I not only honed my skills as a handicapper and punter but also gained invaluable insights into the importance of integrity, perseverance and friendship.

Though Roy may no longer be with us in body, his spirit lives on in every race meeting that I attend, every bet I place, and every victory I celebrate. I miss him every day. His legacy endures as a testament to the profound impact one person can have on another's life, and I am forever grateful for the indelible mark that Roy Reeves left on mine.

In the chapters that follow, I continued to navigate the exhilarating highs and humbling lows of the racing world, drawing strength from the lessons imparted by my dear friend, Roy.

As an owner, I immersed myself in the racing scene. I attended race meetings regularly, where I would meet other owners, trainers, jockeys, and racing enthusiasts who shared my enthusiasm for the sport. Through conversations, shared experiences, and a mutual love for horses, deep friendships began to blossom. These relationships were not solely based on the common interest of horseracing but often extended to personal bonds, support, and shared life experiences. We ventured into horse racing sponsorship, where we sponsored racehorse trainers, and races.

The racetrack became a meeting place for clients. It was a hub of activity where my friends and I would come together to discuss horses, analyse races, and share our triumphs and disappointments. We celebrated victories as a collective, offering each other congratulations and support during moments of success. Likewise, during challenging times, we leaned on one another for encouragement and advice, understanding the highs and lows that come with horse ownership.

Beyond the racetrack, these friendships endured. My racing companions became more than just acquaintances—they became confidants, sharing not only their racing experiences but also their personal lives. We would attend social events together, organise outings, and even supported one another through tough times outside of the racing world.

I am now out of racehorse ownership for several reasons, but the bonds I had formed within the racing community remained strong. My friends continued to be a significant part of my life. They stayed in touch, meeting for meals, gathering to watch races on television, or simply spending time together. Their connection transcended the ownership of horses, as they shared an understanding and appreciation for the sport that had brought us together.

Attending race meetings, even as a spectator now, still holds great meaning for me. It allows me to relive the memories of my ownership days, reminisce about the horses I once had, and catch up with my friends from the racing community. The racetrack serves as a reminder of the excitement, the camaraderie, and the shared passion that defined this chapter of my life.

Exploring the wider world

We loved to Travel to the Canary Islands, and Tenerife was our favourite destination, it not only offered breathtaking landscapes and vibrant cultures but also provided the opportunity to forge lasting friendships with fascinating individuals like

Johnny Malony (AKA) Dublin Johnny. Amidst the clear blue waters and sun-kissed beaches, Johnny's warm Irish charm, and character stood out, earning him the affectionate nickname of "Dublin Johnny" among locals and fellow travellers alike.

Our encounters with Johnny unfolded like chapters in a well-loved novel, each visit to the islands revealing new dimensions to our friendship. Whether regaling us with tales of his homeland over pints of Guinness or leading impromptu excursions to hidden gems off the beaten path, Johnny's zest for life was infectious. His genuine interest in people and knack for storytelling transformed chance encounters into enduring bonds.

Johnny's presence added, and still does today adds an extra layer of magic to our island adventures. From exploring traditional Canarian cuisine at local tavernas and picking out winners to have a little bet on, every moment spent in his company felt like a treasure trove of shared experiences. I am so honoured to have met such a lovely man.

I was a very lucky owner, and I had many winners over the years. The racing world and the connections forged within it remain a cherished part of my story, reminding me of the joy and friendship that can be found in pursuing a shared passion.

This period of my life was the highest that I had ever experienced, I was secure in business, I had a lovely family, and I was supporting my brothers and sister.

Yet fate, had another cruel twist in store for me.

I did not know it but, I was about to hit another low point in my life that was to completely turn my world upside down and ruin me financially.

Chapter 24

Unearthing the Past: The Journey into Forgotten Memories

As I walked the path of life, there were moments when whispers from the past reached out, as if beckoning me to explore the corridors of forgotten memories. It was like hearing distant echoes of laughter, footsteps, and voices that once played prominent roles in the symphony of my life. These echoes were invitations to revisit the experiences that had shaped me.

The journey into the past was not just about revisiting old photographs or places; it was about connecting with the essence of who I once was. It was about understanding the roots that had nurtured my growth. I am reminded of the power of remembrance.

The past is not just a collection of faded images; it is a reservoir of experiences that shape our perception of the world. It is a reminder that every step taken, every decision made, has contributed to the person I am today.

Having worked tirelessly for 40 years, I was about to face one of the biggest challenges in my life!

On the 21st of May 2003, whilst on my way to see a client, I was involved in a near fatal road traffic accident that stopped me in my tracks. I sustained a broken neck in 3 places. Little did I know at the time what that accident would do to me both personally and financially.

I underwent months of treatment, and intense therapy including fighting chronic pain which led to depression.

In the aftermath of the life-altering road traffic accident (R.T.A), my world was shattered, both physically and emotionally. As the broken pieces of my body were painstakingly mended, a darkness began to settle within me, casting a shadow over my spirit. Chronic pain and depression became unwelcome companions, pulling me deeper into a state of despair. I felt for the first time the urge to end my life.

Recognising the urgency of my situation, I sought treatment at a rehab clinic in London. For three months, this sanctuary became my refuge, offering a glimmer of hope amidst the despair that engulfed me. Within the walls of the clinic, I embarked on a journey of healing, guided by a team of compassionate professionals who were determined to help me reclaim my life.

During my time at the clinic, counselling sessions, CBT, became an integral part of my treatment. Sitting face-to-face with a compassionate Psychologists, I began to peel back the layers of my past, confronting the demons that had haunted me for far too long. It was within these courageous conversations that the floodgates of repressed memories were opened, allowing the truth of my experiences to come rushing forth.

As I dug deeper into the recesses of my mind, I was confronted with the stark reality of the abuse I had endured during my time at the orphanage. The memories, long suppressed, rose to the surface, bringing with them a mix of emotions, pain, anger, confusion and sorrow. It was as if a dam had burst, and I was finally able to release the weight that had burdened my soul for 45 years.

Talking openly about my experiences with a compassionate listener proved to be an incredible catalyst for healing. It was as though the walls of silence and shame that had surrounded my past crumbled away, replaced by an empowering sense of liberation and validation. Finally, I felt seen and heard, my pain acknowledged and understood.

Through these transformative conversations, I gained a newfound perspective on the impact of my past on my present. The abuse I had endured had shaped my worldview, influencing the choices I made and the way I navigated through life. But in sharing my story, I discovered that I was not defined by my past, nor was I destined to be a victim forever. I had the power to reclaim my narrative and shape my own future.

The road to healing was not without its challenges. Revisiting the painful memories took immense courage, and there were moments when

I questioned whether I could bear the weight of my past. However, with each conversation, I grew stronger. I learned to lean on the support of my psychologist and the community of fellow survivors, who provided a safe space for me to unravel the complexities of my journey.

Leaving the clinic, I carried with me the tools and insights that would guide me on the path of continued healing. The courage to confront my past and speak my truth had set me free. It was a monumental step towards reclaiming my identity and forging a future that was no longer overshadowed by the scars of my past.

I continue to explore the journey of healing and self-discovery that unfolded in the wake of my time at the rehab clinic. I continued as a day patient for 2 years after leaving.

Thoughts turned to us taking a break from the arduous treatment regime, and my medical consultants had told me that I could go away on holiday, but that I could not fly because of the build-up of pressure in the aeroplane on my spine.

Angie came up with the idea of a cruise. So that was what we did!

Our cruise adventures were not just about seeking exotic destinations and luxury experiences; they were also about extending a helping hand to those in need.

During one of our trips to Africa, we were horrified to see scenes beyond our luxury suite that had a profound impact on us both. The site of hunger and deprivation amongst the indigenous population brought tears to our eyes. Amidst the azure waters and breathtaking landscapes, we found opportunities to connect with local communities and to try and help them to make a tangible difference in their lives.

During one unforgettable journey to South Africa, we felt compelled to answer the call of compassion in a local township near Cape Town. It was here that we witnessed firsthand the stark realities of poverty and deprivation faced by the indigenous people. Determined to make a difference, we rolled up our sleeves and set out to lend a helping hand in whatever way we could. It was against the advice of the cruise operators, who told us that they would not be responsible if anything were to happen to us.

With a spirit of determination and empathy, I organised through local charities a soup kitchen to provide nourishment to those struggling to make ends meet.

The humble act of serving warm meals became a beacon of hope in the lives of the township residents, offering not just sustenance for their bodies but also a sense of dignity and belonging in their community.

Amidst the challenges faced by the township residents, one young man's story touched our hearts in a profound way. Recognising his potential and determination to carve out a better future for his family, I made the decision to sponsor him in learning to drive. It was a small gesture with immense implications, as it opened doors to employment opportunities previously beyond his reach. It also enabled him to continue his education programme.

I purchased a taxi for the young man, providing him with a means to earn a living and support himself and his family. The transformation was nothing short of remarkable, as he embraced his newfound independence with gratitude and determination. The taxi became more than just a mode of transportation; it was a symbol of hope and empowerment for a brighter tomorrow.

Years passed, but the bond forged during our time in South Africa remained steadfast. The young man kept in touch; his letters filled with expressions of gratitude for the opportunity extended to him. His success became a testament to the power of compassion and the transformative impact of a helping hand extended in times of need; it reminded me of the help I had received during my time on the streets all those years ago.

Our experience in Africa taught us that compassion knows no boundaries. Through our small acts of kindness, we witnessed the ripple effect of compassion as it touched and transformed lives in unexpected ways. It was a reminder that every gesture of kindness, no matter how small, has the power to ignite hope and change lives for the better.

I wanted to share another experience that will remain with us for the rest of our lives.

We set sail from Cape Town to Port Louis in Mauritius, the journey took us to Tolagnaro in Madagascar. The cruise ship would do this journey once a month. We recall arriving overnight in Tolagnaro and being woken up early the next morning to the sound of chanting and singing, we soon realised that the local villagers who were on makeshift vessels, which resembled canoes and were surrounding the ship, were asking for money from the passengers.

That morning, we decided to get some dollars from the ship's purser's office.

Angie and I took the tender into Tolagnaro, our shock at seeing hundreds of young mothers, and their children desperately asking, "Please give me dollar for food," to us, as they grabbed at our clothing. They also asked us for our shoes, I gave them my watch and shirt, anything that would help them to get food for their children. We handed out the money to as many families as we could, but it soon ran out. We both took off our shoes and gave them to one family, and the little boy who was in the party danced around as though we had given him the world.

Despite having gained independence from France for more than 50 years, Madagascar continues to endure as one of the world's poorest nations, with 78% of its population living in extreme poverty.

Our journeys around the world were not just about sightseeing and leisure; they were a platform for giving back to the communities we encountered along the way. Inspired by the diverse cultures and landscapes we encountered, we felt compelled to contribute in meaningful ways to the well-being of others. Whether it was through direct involvement in local initiatives or supporting charities from afar, our travels became a conduit for spreading kindness and making a positive impact on the world.

As we traversed continents and explored far-flung destinations, we sought out opportunities to extend a helping hand to those in need, whether it was volunteering at local shelters, participating in community projects, or simply lending a listening ear to those we encountered.

Our commitment to making a difference didn't end with our travels; it extended into our business endeavours as well. Through my business, we made it a priority to support numerous charities with regular donations and ongoing support. From organisations dedicated to alleviating poverty and hunger to those championing, homelessness, and environmental conservation and healthcare initiatives, we sought to be a force for positive change in the world.

Incorporating principles of corporate social responsibility into our business operations, we recognised the profound impact that even small gestures had on improving lives and fostering sustainable change. Whether it was donating a percentage of profits to charitable causes, organising fundraising events, or actively promoting social and environmental causes, we sought to align our business practices with our values of compassion and philanthropy.

As we reflected on our journey of giving, we realised that our actions have the power to inspire others, who read this story, to join us in making a difference. By sharing our experiences and encouraging others to embrace a spirit of generosity and compassion, we hope to create a ripple effect of kindness that would reverberate far beyond our own contributions. In leaving behind a legacy of giving, we aimed to sow the seeds of hope and possibility for a brighter and more compassionate world.

Chapter 25

A Journey of Deceit

Life has its way of bringing you back down to earth. On the other side the feeling of betrayal lay ahead, and we walked straight into it.

We travelled by train to London Bridge in the UK to embark the ship.

It was while I was recuperating on the cruise with Angie, that we first met the four people that would eventually influence every aspect of our lives for the next 25 years, I remember the first night of the cruise. Angie and I had dinner and decided to visit the ship's casino. It was while playing roulette that a man on the opposite side of the table made a derogatory comment to Angie, about me, that was upsetting. I was at the time in a neck brace, and his comment of "how often do you have to feed him" was directed towards us.

The room fell silent! Angie, being Angie, who could be a fiery character replied with a response that put him in his place. He eventually left the casino with his tail between his legs. What we had not observed during all this was that our new friends were also playing roulette, and one of them, a lady, spoke out to Angie and said good on you for putting him in his place. It is hard to imagine that these four individuals who seemed really genuine had a plan and, it was from that Moment on that we were their next victims with their long game plan which in part led me into investing in their various projects, eventually that would lead to us losing everything we owned.

All four of them had a big part to play in our downfall. After the cruise they invited us to stay in their homes in the South of England, and they would buy us expensive gifts. Do not get me wrong, we loved the attention, and we were so pleased to have these new friends in our lives, it was like being romanced and we could not get enough of it. As the months went by, they were getting increasingly friendly, taking us to high end events, and even paying for us to go on the Orient Express.

As time went on, they were getting extremely interested in my business and how investments were made and who ultimately made investment decisions. It was not long before I was asked to attend meetings on their building projects some of which were huge. Including new Five Star Hotels in the South of England.

I was impressed with their property portfolio, and I felt that asking my portfolio of investors to invest was a real opportunity. Investment decisions relating to my Trustee Company were not mine to make, as this was taken out of my hands due to the road traffic accident. The decisions, therefore, were made by the board, which consisted of a lawyer, managing director, and a technical director. All I was able to do was introduce new investors to the team.

I had in place a team of highly qualified and experienced actuaries who ultimately made recommendations to the board on investments. After getting to know our new friends over time, I willingly invested my own money in their property portfolio ventures. I also introduced them to my Trustee Advisers.

They held meetings with the Schemes' Actuaries, and Investment Managers to discuss potential Property Investments. It just so happened around that time that we were negotiating an investment with one of the big four accountancy firms who had an investment opportunity into a French car company Property Development in their new property investment in Romania, that had a guarantee from the car company. In fact, the development was for staff accommodation for the workers' new car production site.

Around the same time, because of my injuries sustained in the RTA, I had decided that I wanted to explore the possibility of passing the business to the existing team. The team did not include the trustee's independent actuary.

I subsequently found out that because of us not involving him in the management buyout of my business, he started to make trouble for the team by challenging decisions that he had previously endorsed. Having given the go-ahead initially, the independent Trustee-appointed actuary some months later without discussing his concerns with either the Trustees or the Investment managers, decided to report himself and my company of trustees to the Regulatory body who regulated my business. Saying at the time that he was no longer confident in the investment returns that he had previously negotiated as a result of investing in the new car production site project, that he had recommended and fully sanctioned.

This resulted in the regulator immediately appointing a new trustee. Their brief was to review the Investment and the Actuaries' concerns. The first I knew about any of this was when I was subjected to Civil litigation, which led to an invasion of my business premises by court-appointed bailiffs searching for documents. I was also subjected to a freezing order. At the same time, searches were being conducted at the premises of our actuaries and investment managers.

I was fully authorised under the trust's deed to invest in investments that I felt were appropriate.

Obtaining a freezing order also allowed the new trustee to remove assets from my business, without us being able to put together our counterarguments.

I was told that I was not allowed to present myself at the court hearing. As they were investigating what they said was a conflict of interest, with individuals who they said were more than just friends.

I had learned at the time that the Judge, initially, would not listen to my team's version of events. They just ploughed on without considering our defence.

Despite my best efforts to provide my side of the story, through the appointment of an extremely expensive firm of London lawyers, it seemed that the new trustee with the support of the regulator was hell-bent in his pursuit of my trustee company.

They were singularly focused on my personal relationships with the people that we had met some years before. They were particularly interested in their property businesses, with whom I had made a number of investments. I also understood at the time that they conducted a separate concurrent investigation into their companies.

The regulators seemed determined to follow their prescribed path, disregarding the complex circumstances of a pension trustee. The impact of their actions was not just professional but deeply personal, affecting the lives and security of many families. It is important that I give a brief explanation as to our responsibilities as Trustees. We had under our control a number of distressed Pension Schemes, with large deficits, often with no future funding capability from Employers. In those cases, The Pension's Regulator would have appointed my firm as trustee, or a similar firm to manage the Pension Schemes.

The investment objective for us as Trustees was somewhat different from a scheme that was ongoing with a solvent employer in place to pick up any cash shortfalls relating to future funding. If a scheme had fallen into a deficit position, the Employer would have had to make up the shortfall.

We, as Trustees, had to adopt a slightly more reactive investment strategy. This was the case in all the schemes under our control. We were fully aware that we had to make some investment decisions that would not have been necessary if the schemes were in a solvent state. We had to consider a more pragmatic approach to our investment strategy and invest in property growth funds (for their potential higher returns). For example, the average returns quoted were circa 9-12% per annum, just what our distressed schemes required to reduce solvency levels. My trustee brief required me to take proactive investment decisions on behalf of the schemes, so given the dire circumstances of the schemes in question, and the need to take urgent investment decisions in order to save the schemes from the pension protection fund and to save the jobs of those scheme members, I made those decisions unreservedly within the guidelines of my trust deeds.

The pension protection fund incidentally is a last resort. It falls on the Government to help preserve an element of the benefits accrued by its members.

My brief was hugely different and almost impossible at times to achieve. I might add here that investment decisions had to be signed off and agreed by the scheme Actuary and its appointed Investment Manager before they could be accepted by the pension Scheme sponsored employer who ultimately had to sanction their implementation. I could not have made investment decisions myself as the trustee!

The terms of the investment in question were for five years with an option to withdraw after an initial period of three years. My Trustee investment objective was to achieve an average return of 8% compound over the first three years as a minimum return if possible. This strategy matched the pension liability profile of the schemes, under our control and was sanctioned by the scheme's independent Actuaries and Company Directors of the schemes.

Chapter 26

Loss of Litigation and our Trust in the Process

Before the Civil case against me was settled, and please understand that I was not allowed to challenge the regulators' findings, "The findings of a whistleblower". I had enough, it went on for over three years, and during that time my business was gone, and my reputation. Along with personal assets.

I had run out of funds to continue challenging them. I was desperate for closure so without taking advice or reading the regulators' settlement letter, I just signed it under duress and sent it back by post. I was receiving treatment for severe depression at the time, and I was on a large dose of anti-depressants. I now know that was the biggest mistake of my life.

Three months after agreeing to settle, I received correspondence from the new Trustee firm appointed by the Regulator, that they withdrew their allegations against me and my Trustee Company. They had confirmed that the investments made by my Trustee Company were, in fact, "safe" and did meet all the standards required as a Pension Trustee. So, what does that mean? They lied, Angie and I lost everything.

(Here again is there not a question of Professional Negligence against both the Regulators and the New Trustee, also the London Lawyers who acted for the trustee for the loss of my overall business, and personal assets?) The facts are that the investments that were made by my trustee company were permitted investments and were within the rules of my trust deed as a Pension Trustee and in fact were remarkably successful. It goes to show that someone who has a grudge against another person has the power to completely ruin their lives, without investigation. The question of assets: the freezing order was made against all personal and business assets which included Angie's assets who had nothing to do with the original pension regulators' challenge against my business. She was not an officer of the business nor was she an employee of the trustee firm.

Compensation for my RTA (Road Traffic Accident), May 2003

Some years before this action I had received Compensation because of an RTA road traffic accident. I had a Coutts bank account, with over £1 million which was awarded to me as a result of personal injuries sustained by me in that RTA. That £1 million Fund was for my future. I do not and did not at the time think that this money should have been taken from me, as it was paid for my injuries and was not part of my business. Clarification had been given by the firm of Solicitors who represented me in that compensation claim. I believe this to be correct and at worst I should be able to reclaim that money.

An Independent Barrister Opinion: I also paid for an independent pension Barrister's Opinion during the Civil litigation against me. This stated that indeed, I was not conflicted in my actions as a Trustee. The opinion also examined the question of remuneration and if my trust company was allowed under the trust deeds to be remunerated from investments made on schemes under our management, by third parties. For example, if a fund manager paid us for placing a piece of business with that organisation, we would have received a commission/fee for placing that investment with that organisation. That was how we got remunerated as there was no employer to pay us fees. We were remunerated by placing investments.

The question was a precise one because further into the actions against me which was offered later in the litigation by the new trustees and the pension's regulator once the freezing order had been granted, "The opinion clearly stated that doing my duties as trustee entitled me to be remunerated by my trust." This was borne out in the trust deeds and it went on further to say that "payments through third parties were allowed provided that this remuneration did not deplete the pension Trust Funds", which it did not! This was further supported by the scheme Actuary who had to sign off all ins and outs relating to the scheme's funds.

I had strong reasons to believe that it was not in my interests to involve other parties in trying to defend my trust company's position. I was questioned at great length by the regulators, it soon became clear from the initial questioning made by the investigators, and other parties, that they were keen for others to be included in their overall investigations. Navigating this situation required immense strength and resilience. I had to find a delicate balance between cooperating with the regulators to the extent that I felt comfortable and safe.

The following 3 years of their investigations were a constant battle of priorities, with the weight of responsibility on my shoulders. The lawyers I engaged on my behalf sought to take advantage of the many millions of pounds of my money that was at their disposal in my bank account to run up huge fees that resulted in cozy conversations with the newly appointed regulator trustees who did their utmost to discredit me.

It was not long before the money had run out, and the ability to keep funding my defence was no longer there. That is injustice. So, the Lawyers decided that they could not continue defending me and suggested that I looked at alternatives such as 'no win no fee' firms. I felt that the time had come for me to not challenge the regulators' findings. It resulted in me being struck off as a forensic consultant and trustee. It meant that my ability to work in the financial sector was taken away from me without the case being proved against me or my business.

The experience served as a stark reminder of the lengths I was willing to go to protect what truly mattered to me, even in the face of overwhelming obstacles and challenges. Looking back in hindsight on the situation, I should have taken a different course of action and challenged the findings of the regulators.

The confiscation of all my personal assets, and those of my wife, Angie, which represented 30 years of hard work and financial success, was a significant blow that left a lasting impact. While it still occasionally grates me on what could have been, I also understand that dwelling on the past will not change the outcome. My own personal losses amounted to many millions of pounds, all lost in a property investment in Scotland, that I had invested in with our so-called four friends.

I have come to accept that my family's security and happiness are more important than material possessions. I came from nothing, and I remain determined to create a brighter future for them, using the lessons learned from this experience to navigate the challenges that lie ahead.

However, despite this setback, my resilience and determination kicked in. Again, I refused to let these circumstances define me or break my spirit. With sheer determination, I have set out to rebuild my life again from scratch, reverting back to my experiences as a child and the days spent sleeping on the streets. It was a challenging journey, filled with setbacks and obstacles, but I refused to give up.

I have learned valuable lessons about trust, and I feel bitterly disappointed by the way that the system once again had let me down. I had learned the importance of protecting my own interests and would not be fooled again.

The reality of losing everything that I had worked so hard for was undoubtedly daunting and disheartening. I had invested years of effort, sweat, and dedication into building my assets and achieving financial success.

Nevertheless, I held onto the belief that true wealth resided in the love, support, and resilience of my family, rather than in material possessions. I drew strength from the unwavering bond we shared and the ability to weather any storm together. The loss of assets served as a catalyst for revaluating my priorities, placing greater emphasis on the intangible riches that money could never buy.

Learning to live with the guilt and the shame of falling foul of unscrupulous advisers, and a regulatory system, and letting down both family and friends was an emotional burden that weighed heavily on me and continues to do so.

Guilt and shame are two distinct but related emotions. The guilt came from the belief that I had deliberately done wrong or harmful to others, while the shame and embarrassment or disgrace related to my actions. In my case, me falling victim to four individuals who had befriended Angie and me, whom we put our utmost trust in triggered feelings of guilt for me not preventing it.

I was told that it is common for individuals who have lost everything to blame themselves, even though they are victims. I now realise that we were targeted because of our trust, not because of any personal failing.

Dealing with the guilt and shame can be isolating.

I have used this experience as an opportunity to gain experience and grow. I now know what red flags were missed and how to protect myself and others in the future. By becoming more aware and informed, I have regained a sense of control. Forgiving oneself was the most challenging step.

I have learned the art of self-compassion by treating myself with the same kindness and understanding that I would offer to a friend facing a similar situation. It is okay to make mistakes; what matters is how we learn and grow from them.

Moving Forward

Life is a series of experiences, both positive and negative. It is crucial to recognise that our worth and identity are not defined by one event. You have the power to shape your future and create new, positive narratives.

⊷⊷◁❰◆❱▷⊷⊷

Chapter 27

Weathering Life's Turbulences

Life, like nature, has its storms. In this chapter, I invite you to step into the tempests I have faced and the lessons I have learned from surviving them. These trials have moulded me, revealing the strength within and the resilience that emerges when faced with life's greatest challenges.

The storms in life often arrive unannounced, like dark clouds rolling in on a sunny day. These tumultuous beginnings can bring chaos and uncertainty, evaluating the foundations we have built and shaking our sense of security. In these moments, it is easy to feel overwhelmed, but I have learned that storms can also be teachers, revealing our capacity to endure and adapt.

Loss, like a torrential downpour, can flood our lives with grief and pain. The rain of tears may seem never-ending, but amidst the deluge, we find the strength to grieve, to mourn what was, and eventually to find a new path. Surviving such storms requires leaning on the pillars of support that surround us – friends, family, and the inner resilience that carries us through.

Amid my life's storm, I discovered the ability to withstand the harshest of circumstances and emerge stronger. Just as lightning illuminates the darkest skies, resilience can light our way through the most challenging times. It is a force that teaches us to bend without breaking, to find solutions where there seem to be none, and to embrace change when change is necessary.

As the storm subsides, we are left to assess the damage and begin the process of rebuilding. But amidst the debris, there is an opportunity for renewal. Just as after a forest fire, new growth emerges, I found that rebuilding after life's storms can lead to transformation. The process of rebuilding not only restores what was lost but can also reveal new strengths, new perspectives and new directions.

The storms I have faced have taught me that survival is a symphony. It is the harmonious interplay of endurance, courage, and hope. It is finding strength during chaos and embracing vulnerability while standing resilient. Just as the symphony builds to a crescendo before subsiding into harmony, surviving life's storms is a journey of crescendos and decrescendos – of navigating the tumultuous moments and finding peace of mind in the calm that follows.

The result of losing everything resulted in me being declared bankrupt. I found myself facing a devastating loss. Circumstances beyond my control led to the unravelling of my fortune, leaving me bankrupt and homeless once again. It was a crushing blow, shattering the foundation that I had painstakingly built.

I was unaware of the devastation bankruptcy would cause me. It took a toll on every aspect of my life. The financial setback left me feeling trapped and restricted, as I faced the challenges of rebuilding from the ground up. Living day to day became a struggle, as I grappled with the consequences of my financial downfall. It bought shame upon me, and my family. I felt degraded, and embarrassed and helpless.

The denial of credit impacted every aspect of my daily life. It affected my ability to make purchases or invest in opportunities that could potentially help me rebuild a basic credit rating. I did not realise that the limitations placed upon me would hinder my progress and created a sense of frustration and helplessness. It was a challenge to secure a rental property because no landlord wants a bankrupt as a tenant. With advice from a close solicitor friend, I reluctantly changed my name, from Michael Gerard Conway to Gerard Conway. It allowed me to at least speak to people without the door being shut in my face as soon as I mentioned my real name.

I found it almost impossible to get a stable place to call home. If it wasn't for my youngest daughter, Julie, who let us live in her house, we would also have been made homeless.

Despite my best efforts to regain stability, the bankruptcy record continued to haunt me, making it difficult to secure any financial support or to obtain credit for essential needs. This added layer of frustration and limitation served as a constant reminder of my past struggles and the uphill battle I faced in regaining my financial footing.

Living with the consequences of bankruptcy also brought emotional and psychological challenges. I had to navigate feelings of shame, embarrassment, and disappointment; along with that I fell into a state of severe depression. I grappled with the notion of failure and wrestled with self-doubt. The weight of the situation often felt overwhelming, and I had to summon all my resilience to keep moving forward.

I flatly refused to let my circumstances define me. It was like the days of being on the streets, I thought to myself often. That I had no credit rating back in those days. It made me tap into my inner strength and determination, using the experience as a catalyst for growth and personal transformation. I sought guidance and looked at self-employed cash in hand jobs.

With time, persistence, and a plan in place, I have gradually started to get my life back on track.

I embraced opportunities of professional development, expanding my skill set and seizing new areas for success. Through sheer determination and unwavering resolve, I have demonstrated to myself how resilience and ability helps overcome adversity.

Please, do not get me wrong; it was one of the hardest things I have had to do.

The experience served as a powerful reminder for me to be more discerning in my business dealings and to prioritise my own well-being and financial security. It was a painful lesson I had to be cautious in my approach to both business and personal relationships.

The isolation from so-called friends, who seemed to vanish when I needed support the most, was a stark reality.

However, amidst this challenging time, there was one true friend, Darren Vernon, who stood by me unwaveringly. Darren offered his wholehearted support, lending a compassionate ear and providing financial assistance when times were particularly tough. His steadfast presence and genuine care were a beacon of light during a dark period, demonstrating the essence of true friendship and solidarity. I am pleased to say that Darren is still a friend today.

It was ironic that those I had once helped in their times of need were nowhere to be found when the tables turned. In moments of adversity, it became clear that true support came from family, the ones who knew the reality of the situation.

The process of rebuilding demanded not only challenging work but also a willingness to adapt, a challenging task at the age of 64. However, with the right attitude, I discovered that even starting from the bottom was achievable. The isolation from fair-weather friends became an opportunity to surround myself with those who truly mattered, the ones who stood by me during the storm.

The path to regaining stability was a journey of constant learning, I had to adapt to the challenges of reinventing myself later in life, but the determination to overcome them proved to be a powerful driving force. The experience taught me that age should never be a barrier to starting again. With the right mindset, even the most significant setbacks could be overcome.

Beginning anew at the age of 64 was a humbling experience. It required a shift in perspective and a commitment to growth that went beyond the conventional boundaries of age. The journey taught me that resilience and a positive attitude were the cornerstones of achieving success, regardless of the circumstances.

The experience of loss and subsequent rebuilding had transformed me into a wiser and more empathetic individual. The pain of isolation had etched a deeper understanding of the value of genuine connections and the importance of discerning loyal friends from those who merely thrived in fair weather.

Through the arduous process of rebuilding, I developed a profound appreciation for hard-earned success. The setbacks had refined my character, instilling in me a deeper sense of gratitude for every achievement, no matter how small.

The restoration of financial stability marked only one aspect of my journey. Beyond that, it rekindled a sense of purpose within me. The scars became a source of strength, propelling me to engage in philanthropic endeavours and community involvement. The mission was clear: to make a positive impact in the lives of others who, like me, had faced the harsh realities of life.

The long journey back from the depths of despair had not only restored my individual stability but also paved the way for a legacy of triumph and resilience.

The lessons learned, the challenges overcome, and the newfound purpose created a narrative that went beyond personal success, resonating in the lives of those touched by the generosity and empathy forged through life's experiences.

Amidst the trials and tribulations, I unearthed a treasure far more valuable than any financial gain—true wealth in the understanding from my family. When life threw its harshest challenges my way, it was the unwavering support and empathy from my family that provided solace and strength. In their understanding eyes, I discovered a richness that transcended material possessions.

Chapter 28

The Full Value of Family

Today, with my wife Angie, my children, Lisa, Philip, and Julie, and my grandchildren Connor, Charlie, Harry, and Sebastian, by my side, I breathe a deep sense of ease. The anxiety that once accompanied the pursuit of wealth and success has been replaced by the tranquility found in the simple joys of family life. It is in their collective presence that I discover a sanctuary, a place where judgment is replaced by understanding, and love is the currency that truly matters.

Through the rollercoaster of my life, I have come to realise having family is the most important thing. It is the anchor that grounds us in times of storm and the lighthouse guiding us through life's rough seas.

The journey, though challenging, has been a lesson in rediscovering life's true essence. In the embrace of family, I have found the greatest wealth—a wealth of love, understanding, and shared moments. Through the highs and lows, it is the reassurance that comes from the laughter of my grandchildren.

As I navigate the later chapters of my life, I understand that the legacy I leave behind is not solely financial or professional. It is the legacy of family love and empathy—the kind that withstands storms and shines brightly even in the darkest hours. In the warmth of familial bonds, I have discovered an enduring wealth that transcends time and circumstance.

Our daughter, Julie, the youngest of our children rescued us and bought a house for the 3 of us to live in. I can't tell you how upsetting it was for Angie and me to be facing destitution at this stage of our lives. Thank God for our daughter.

The gesture from our youngest daughter, Julie, was nothing short of a lifeline in our darkest hour. As we found ourselves facing the cruel reality of homelessness once again, her act of compassion and generosity shone like a beacon of hope amidst the despair. It was a gesture that spoke volumes about the depth of her love and the unwavering bond of family.

In the midst of our dire circumstances, Julie's selfless act of rescuing us from destitution took on a profound significance. It was proof of her empathy and kindness, a reflection of the values instilled in her by her upbringing.

Despite the challenges we faced, we were blessed to have a daughter who not only cared about us but was willing to take decisive action to ensure our well-being.

As we settled into the home that Julie had bought for us all, the overwhelming sense of relief washed over us like a warm embrace. It was a place of sanctuary, a tangible reminder of the love and support that surrounded us, even in our darkest hour.

We knew that no matter what challenges lay ahead, we would face them together as a family, united by a bond that could weather any storm.

Looking back on that pivotal Moment, I am filled with an overwhelming sense of gratitude for our daughter's selfless act of kindness. Her generosity not only provided us with a roof over our heads but also restored our faith in humanity and reminded us of the power of love.

Having a home had given me a new lease of life once again. So, I put myself out there and found paid work, for which I was so grateful. It was the first rung of a tall ladder that I had started to climb. During this time, I also helped my daughter Julie start her own business. That gave me great satisfaction to be able to support her in the journey that hopefully will be another success story.

With gratitude swelling in my heart, I set out to find paid work, eager to prove myself and contribute to our household once more. Each job application I submitted, each interview I attended, showed my determination to turn my life around. And when I finally received that long-awaited phone call offering me a consultant's role, I felt a surge of pride and gratitude wash over me. I was totally honest with everyone, and I explained at interviews my reasons for changing my name to Gerard.

My journey didn't stop there. In addition to focusing on my own career advancement, I also found fulfilment in supporting my daughter Julie as she embarked on her own entrepreneurial journey. Together, we worked tirelessly to turn her business idea into a reality, drawing upon our combined skills and experiences to navigate the challenges of entrepreneurship.

In the end, my journey from homelessness to newfound stability was not just about overcoming adversity; it was about embracing the opportunities that life presented and finding peace in the journey itself.

"Reflecting on the journey of the past few years, there's one pivotal Moment that stands out vividly in my mind—a Moment that not only altered the course of my professional life but also rejuvenated my spirit with a renewed sense of hope and purpose.

It was during one of our visits to a new company lead, four years ago, when fate led me to encounter a man whose name now resonates deeply within me—Mike Forster. From the Moment we met, there was an instant connection, a resonance that transcended mere professional acquaintance. Mike, the business owner of an esteemed Engineering company, exuded warmth, integrity, and an unwavering passion for his craft.

As our encounters grew in frequency over the following three years, our rapport blossomed into a genuine friendship rooted in mutual respect and shared aspirations. It was during this time, amidst conversations where I bared my soul and shared the challenges weighing heavily upon me, that Mike, in his characteristic generosity of spirit, extended a hand of opportunity unlike any I had experienced before.

With unwavering trust and belief in my abilities, Mike offered me a role integral to his business—a consultancy position that not only promised professional growth but also served as a beacon of hope in what had seemed like a sea of uncertainty. His gesture, laden with faith and confidence, was a Moment that transcended mere professional transactions—it was a lifeline, a gesture of genuine goodwill that breathed new life into my dreams.

Mike's act of kindness and belief in me is a treasure I hold dear—a testament to the transformative power of human connection and the profound impact one individual can have on another's life journey. For his unwavering support, his belief in my potential, and the opportunity he bestowed upon me, I am profoundly grateful.

To Mike, with deepest gratitude, I extend my heartfelt appreciation for the faith you placed in me and the opportunity you bestowed. Your kindness has not only shaped my professional trajectory but has also ignited a flame of hope and determination within me—a flame that will continue to illuminate my path as I journey forward.

Thank you, Mike, for being the beacon of light that guided me through the shadows, and for reminding me that amidst life's challenges, there exists boundless potential for growth, resilience, and new beginnings."

As I looked towards the horizon, I felt a renewed sense of hope and optimism for the road ahead.

Chapter 29

Currently in the Year 2024

Reaching the age of 67, I've come to a profound realisation about life's intricate balance and the universal principle of cause and effect. It's a Moment of clarity where I've grasped the gospel truth that what we put out into the world inevitably finds its way back to us, much like the cyclical rhythm of nature. This understanding underscores the importance of cultivating positivity, kindness, and empathy in our interactions, knowing that these seeds will eventually bear fruit in our lives and in thc lives of others.

Most important is, I have come to understand that the pursuit of happiness often leads us on a quest for an elusive "magic dream" that we have carried since childhood. This dream, whether it's material success, love, or fulfilment, occupies our thoughts and propels us forward in life. Yet, with age comes the wisdom to recognise that true contentment is not found in the attainment of external goals alone. It lies in the richness of our experiences, the depth of our connections, and the moments of joy and gratitude we find along the way.

Life's journey has taught me that true equilibrium isn't about achieving a state of perfect balance, but rather about navigating the ebbs and flows with grace and resilience. It's about embracing the highs and lows, the triumphs and setbacks, knowing that each Moment carries its own lessons and opportunities for growth.

As I reflect on these insights, I invite readers to join me in embracing the wisdom that comes with age, recognising the interconnectedness of our actions, and cherishing the beauty of life's imperfect but wondrous tapestry. For in this realisation lies the key to living a life of purpose, fulfilment and meaning, regardless of our age or circumstances.

⁕⊷◄〈〉►⊶⁕

Chapter 30

In the End Hope Prevails

In the twilight of my life, as I look back on the winding road I've travelled, I realise that it's not the destination that defines us, but the journey itself. My life has been a tapestry woven from threads of adversity and triumph, heartbreak, and resilience. From the depths of despair to the heights of success, I have witnessed the remarkable capacity of the human spirit to endure, to persevere, and to rise above what is put in front of us.

In the end, this book is not just my story; it confirms the strength of the human mind. It is a reminder that no matter how dark the night may seem, there is always a dawn waiting to break. It is an ode to the love of family, the bonds of friendship, and the power of determination.

As I close the story of my life so far, I am filled with gratitude for the lessons learned, the people met, and the moments cherished. Life has a way of surprising us, of testing our resolve, and of revealing our true selves. And so, as I say farewell to these pages, I invite you, to reflect on your own journey.

May you find inspiration in the stories shared here, the triumphs celebrated, and the challenges overcome. Remember that your life is a narrative in the making, a tale waiting to be told.

Embrace each chapter, for it is through adversity that we discover our strength, and it is through resilience that we find a way out.

Thank you for joining me on my voyage. As the final page turns, let it be a reminder that, no matter where life takes you, your story is worth telling, your voice worth sharing, and your dreams worth chasing.

With hope in my heart and the future on my horizon, I'll say a last goodbye, and wish you a life filled with adventure, love, and the unwavering belief that, no matter the obstacles, your story will always be worth telling."

Author: Gerard Conway

Milton Keynes UK
Ingram Content Group UK Ltd.
UKHW010949260624
444734UK00004B/292